NATIONAL INSECURITY

A Primer on the First Book of Samuel

Keith Bodner

CLEMENTS PUBLISHING
Toronto

Published 2003 by Clements Publishing
6021 Yonge Street, Suite 213
Toronto, Ontario M2M 3W2 Canada
www.clementspublishing.com

National Library of Canada Cataloguing in Publication Data

Bodner, Keith, 1967-
    National insecurity: a primer on the first book of Samuel / Keith Bodner.

Includes bibliographical references.
ISBN 1-894667-29-8

    1. Bible. O.T. Samuel, 1st—Criticism, interpretation, etc. I. Title.

BS1325.3.C63 2003   222'.4305209   C2003-901016-3

CONTENTS

CONTENTS

ACKNOWLEDGEMENTS

There have been some very assiduous commentators on 1 Samuel, and I have benefited from the sensitivity and outstanding scholarship of a number of very fine writers. The work of rigorous academics such as Robert Polzin, J. P. Fokkelman, Peter Miscall, Robert Alter, Barbara Green, Lyle Eslinger, and Walter Brueggemann is immensely rewarding to study, and makes my task both easier and harder. It is rendered an easy labor because of the ground-breaking research and careful scrutiny of the text by these scholars, yet at the same time it is harder because of many difficult issues and questions that they raise. There are certainly other questions which 1 Samuel raises, but the questions I raise in this book are some that I intend to pursue in future studies. I have tried to acknowledge these and other scholars along the way in this book, and endeavored to provide a flavor of their work through various quotations. In the bibliography at the end of this book I have compiled a list of sources that I have found helpful, and the earnest reader is continually encouraged to consult these materials.

Thanking various individuals is invariably problematic, and more names are omitted than included. Although there are many folks who deserve a word of thanks, I can only mention a few here. Rob Clements is a fine editor and colleague, and I applaud his vision for the Christian mind in "our home and native land." A host of students at various institutions, including the University of Aberdeen, Regent College, Briercrest Seminary, and Tyndale College have discussed these issues with me, and I am grateful. Many translation issues were discussed at length in Tyndale's recent Advanced Hebrew class, and I appreciate the perseverance of Brad Johnson, Lloyd Lehrbass, Chris Lortie (Calebite!), Nathan Martin, Matthew McKean, Leo DiSiqueira (Balaam!), Jon Valentin, Mike Weldon, Sam Chung and Roscoe Lancelot Lim. Emmanuel Bible College and McMaster Divinity College have also invited me to teach courses on 1 Samuel, and I am grateful for their support of this work.

Among the many colleagues who have offered support, I must thank Robert Polzin for consistent encouragement, Barbara Green for a very generous spirit and her willingness to share proof copies of her outstanding new book on 1 Samuel, and Gary Knoppers for his many patient conversations around complex issues of the "Deuteronomistic History" and beyond. Members of my local reading community include Richard Davis, Brian Stiller and Timothy Larsen, and I am deeply indebted to Katy Darley, Marina Hofman, and Tim den Broeder for assistance along the way.

My wife Coreen and I would like to dedicate this little book to the Sweetman family (George, Denise, Taylor, Conor, Bradley, Caitlin, and Kieran), occupants of "no ordinary hole" who are skilled readers of difficult narratives. It strikes me that their counter-cultural spirituality is something that the author of 1 Samuel would smile on, which is high praise indeed. They provide a marvelous example of an urban family who take seriously the Incarnation, Death, and Resurrection of the Messiah, and embody the sacrificial commitment and self-denial which is at the heart of the gospel. If 1 Samuel is an indictment on self-aggrandizement, then my reading is profoundly affected by this postmodern household that does not abide by the rules of prevailing culture.

A VERY BRIEF INTRODUCTION

The Old Testament book of 1 Samuel is often underrated in terms of its narrative drama and theological substance. As an attempt to convey the richness and endless subtlety of this biblical book, the present volume provides a free translation of 1 Samuel, with a series of questions and points for reflection following each chapter. These points explore various literary and theological issues raised by the text, including: the introduction of kingship in Israel, the office of the prophet, and the contours of leadership for God's people. Various questions include: why does the nation reject "divine kingship" and opt for a monarchy? Why is Saul rejected? Is Samuel an unbiased prophet? What are the qualities in the young David that set him apart as a king? What dynamics of human relationships are emphasized in the text? The questions in this book provide ample opportunity for reflection on the nature of biblical narrative, the portraits of key personalities, and the profound level of artistic and theological sophistication in this important stretch of biblical material.

By any measure, the story of Israel is a highly compelling drama. It begins with the westward journey of Abram, whose family drifts toward Egypt as the book of Genesis concludes. These disparate ranks of slaves and shepherds are liberated by a mighty act of emancipation, and come to occupy their "land of promise"—where they grow to become a nation and a kingdom before experiencing the grim realities of invasion and exile at the hand of foreign adversaries. This could well mark the end of Israel's history, yet arguably this period of exile and loss leaves the community of God's people with a stronger sense of his transcendence and sovereignty.

The subject of this present study is one component within this larger story, the book known as "1 Samuel." Clearly it is part of a larger work, yet there are numerous reasons for carefully reading it and attending to its details. 1 Samuel is part of a grand narrative that scholars have often termed "the Deuteronomistic History," with the recognition that the biblical books from Joshua-Kings tell a coherent story of Israel's occupation of the promised land from entry to exile. Notably, at the beginning of this narrative (Joshua), the nation is "outside" of the land, and at the end of the narrative (2 Kings) once more the nation is "outside." In between lies a highly complex work of theology. One of the primary purposes of this grand narrative is to tell the story of Israel's experiment with kingship. To paraphrase Barbara Green (2000, chapter 2), 1 Samuel presents a sustained meditation on leadership and the introduction of the monarchy in Israel, and tells the story of "the beginning of kingship after the end of its existence."

1 Samuel is a book that constitutes a very important chapter in Israel's story, since this book narrates the transition from Israel's tribal confederacy to a more centralized statehood and monarchy. The birth of *kingship* is recounted in these pages, and this institution proves pivotal in the life of the nation. The highly-nuanced theology that is articulated in this book reveals that the author of 1 Samuel was persuaded that the community *needed* to seriously reflect on the issues raised in these chapters. To that end, this present study aims to ask a series of literary and theological questions that may prove helpful for an overall reading of 1 Samuel. There are, of course, many more questions that can be asked, and interested readers are directed to the wealth of commentaries, monographs, and scholarly articles on this subject. But the "points for reflection" in this study are designed to challenge and even unsettle a casual reading of the book, and direct the reader to other angles which may not have been previously considered. This is the

primary purpose for the "translation" provided here. It is certainly not a carefully documented philological or text-critical analysis, but rather an example of the way that I often read 1 Samuel. So at times the translation may seem awkwardly literal (to bring about a sense of the original syntax when called for), and at other times closer to paraphrase, as an attempt to recreate the vividness, beauty, and delightful ambiguities of Hebrew prose, and the collage of images that are formed in the reader's mind. Any translation is necessarily provisional, and my gloss of 1 Samuel in this study is certainly no exception. It is expected that readers of this book will continually consult other translations and versions and explore points of difference. I have endeavored to work with the Masoretic Hebrew text (as opposed to variant readings in the Greek Septuagint or Qumran fragments) as much as possible, even when the sense of a particular word or phrase is obscure. The Hebrew text of 1 Samuel is notoriously difficult in places, and the advanced reader is directed to professional commentaries and encouraged to carefully weigh such matters. This study preserves the traditional "chapter" divisions as a practical reading device, but eschews "verses," since they can be a potential hindrance.

1 Samuel contains a wealth of intriguing personalities who dominate the landscape of the book. The prophet Samuel looms large in the narrative, and as we will discover, is even *larger than life after death*. Some traditional readings have rather blithely understood the prophet Samuel as a hero, and Israel's first king, Saul as a villain. This kind of reductive reading is not affirmed in this study; rather, it seems that the author of this book paints a more highly sophisticated work of art on this narrative canvas than is often acknowledged. It would seem that 1 Samuel presents a meditation on the office of the prophet even as it unfolds the story of kingship. Saul is certainly a flawed leader who makes his share of blunders (and is guilty of some heinous crimes along the way),

but the reader should keep in mind that the office of "the king" is one that perhaps should not have been created in the first place, and is a job for which Saul did not apply. Is Saul a *tragic hero* in the sense that the ancient Greeks might have understood, or is he stubborn and disobedient? Such questions will be pondered in this study. Moreover, the young David is often rather exclusively referred to as "a man after God's own heart," even as his rather obvious blemishes are discreetly overlooked. To be sure, the outstanding qualities of the young David merit much reflection, but a careful reading of the text must account for some shrewd and politically calculating behavior on David's part. If, as Robert Alter argues at length, David is perhaps the most highly developed figure in ancient literature, it stands to reason that his character will not be banal and flat, but rather multi-dimensional, colorful, diverse, and at times unfathomable.

Finally, our "points for reflection" at the conclusion of each chapter also include the theological dimension of the narrative. How is the institution of kingship presented? Is the message of 1 Samuel that kingship is inherently evil because it involves a rejection of God's kingship over Israel? What, for that matter, is the LORD's view of kingship for his people? How does kingship relate to "covenant"? What do the various episodes impart to its audiences about the character of God, his involvement with the world, and his relationship to his people and the larger world? Furthermore, as a default setting, a reader can always have in mind this question: how would an exile in Babylon read this text? If we appreciate the possibility that a book like 1 Samuel was composed, among other reasons, to explain to the exiles *why* they are in Babylon, such a construct may open some doors of perception for our readings of this book. The community may well be asking, "Why are we in exile?" and 1 Samuel provides a response to part of that puzzle. Israel is continually faced with a host of "national insecurities" in

10

their history: does God really reign over the nations? Is he really involved? Does he care? What is the best way to live our lives should we ever return to the promised land? Is there any messianic impulse in 1 Samuel? The reader should keep in mind a host of possible questions as this endlessly subtle text is confronted, absorbed, and continually re-read. And so begins our journey.

CHAPTER 1

OPENING MOMENTS

Once there was a man from "Twin Heights," of the hill country of Ephraim, and his name was Elkanah, the son of Jeroham, the son of Elihu, the son of Tohu, the son of Zuph, an Ephraimite. He had two wives: the name of the first was Hannah, and the name of second was Peninnah. And for Peninnah there were children, but for Hannah there were no children.

Now every year this man would go up from his city to worship and to sacrifice to the LORD of hosts at Shiloh. It was there that the two sons of Eli, Hophni and Phinehas, were priests of the LORD. And on the day Elkanah sacrificed, he would give portions to Peninnah his wife, and to all her sons and daughters. But to Hannah he could only give a single portion, for he loved Hannah, but the LORD had closed her womb.

However, her rival-wife would intensely provoke her in order to cause her to thunder, because the LORD had closed up her womb. Thus it would happen year after year—as often as she went up to the house of the LORD—that she would provoke her. And she wept, and would not eat. And Elkanah her husband said to her, "Hannah, why do you weep? Why don't you eat? Why is your heart so bad? Aren't I better than ten sons for you?"

And Hannah arose after the eating in Shiloh and after the drinking. Now Eli the priest was sitting on the throne near the doorpost of the LORD's temple. But she was bitter of soul, and she prayed to the LORD and wept inconsolably. She made a vow, and she said, "O LORD of hosts, if you will please look on the affliction of your handmaiden, and if you will remember and not forget her, and if you will give your handmaiden male offspring, then I will give him to the LORD all the days of his life, and a razor will never come on his head."

Now it happened as she intensified her prayer before the LORD, that Eli was watching her mouth. But Hannah was speaking in her heart; while her lips were quivering, her voice was not being heard. And Eli reckoned that she was drunk, and so he said to her, "For how long will you be drunk? Turn aside your wine from you!" Hannah answered and said, "No, my lord, I am a hard-spirited woman! I have not been drinking wine nor liquor, rather I have been pouring out my soul before the LORD. Don't ascribe your handmaiden as a daughter of Belial, because out of the multitude of my complaint and provocation I've been speaking until now." Eli answered and said, "Go in peace, and may the God of Israel grant your request which you have asked (שאל) of him." And she said, "May your maid-servant continue to find grace in your eyes." Then the woman went on her way, and she ate, and her face was not *as it had been* again.

And they arose early in the morning, worshipped before the LORD, returned and went to their house at Ramah. Elkanah knew Hannah his wife, and the LORD remembered her. And when the days came around, Hannah conceived, and gave birth to a son. She called his name "Samuel," because "from the LORD I requested him."

And Elkanah the husband went up with all his household to offer to the LORD the annual sacrifice and his vow. But Hannah did not go up, for she said to her husband, "Only when the lad is weaned will I bring him, that he may appear in the presence of the LORD and live there forever." Her husband Elkanah said to her, "Do what is good in your eyes—stay until you have weaned him—only may the LORD establish *his* word." And the woman stayed and nursed her son until weaning him. So she brought him up with her—*after* she had weaned him—along with three bulls, one ephah of flour and a skin of wine. She brought him to the house of the LORD at Shiloh, and the lad was a retainer.

And they slaughtered the bull, and brought the lad to Eli. And she said, "Oh, my lord, as you live my lord, I'm the woman who was standing next to you here, to pray to the LORD! For this lad I prayed, and the LORD gave me my request which I asked from him. Hence, I also have dedicated him to the LORD; all of the days he has, he is dedicated to the LORD." And there he worshipped the LORD.

POINTS FOR REFLECTION:

1. The book of 1 Samuel opens with an "opening," the opening of Hannah's barren womb, as she gives birth to boy. Notice that this book commences with a genealogy, illustrating that Elkanah is from a stable family line, and while perhaps not illustrious, is of solid stock in Israel. It is interesting that this entire narrative—concerned with the weighty matters of Israel's future leadership—commences with a focus on a family. Why is it that genealogies feature so prominently in the Bible? Hannah, through the condition of barrenness, is effectively excluded from Elkanah's genealogy, and hence excluded from continued fruitfulness in this family line. Ironically, Ephraim means "doubly fruitful," a subtle allusion to the notion of "fruitfulness" which permeates this genealogical line. But what about Hannah? Will she contribute to the fruitfulness of "twice fruitful (Ephraim)"? Note Walter Brueggemann's (1989: 12) comment:

The problem is clearly and immediately articulated. The

man with his impressive genealogy (v. 1) is matched to a barren woman (v. 2). From his fathers, Elkanah has a proud past. With his wife, however, he has no future. The story invites us with Israel to reflect on the question: How is a new future possible amid the barrenness that renders us bitter, hopeless, and fruitless? The dramatic answer to this question is articulated in [the next] four scenes.

2. The narrative makes it clear that Elkanah is a devout citizen, and makes annual worship in Shiloh a priority. Yet in the midst of the ritual of worship, *rivalry* is present. Why is the biblical writer keen on portraying Hannah in the midst of domestic conflict? Are there any allusions to the book of Genesis here? If so, what do such echoes suggest? Evaulate Robert Alter's (1999: 3) comment:

> The reference to two wives, one childbearing, the other childless, immediately alerts the audience to the unfolding of the familiar annunciation type-scene. The expected series of narrative motifs of the annunciation type-scene is: the report of the wife's barrenness (amplified by the optional motif of the fertile co-wife less loved by the husband than is the childless wife); the promise, through oracle or divine messenger or man of God, of the birth of a son; cohabitation resulting in conception and birth. As we shall see, the middle motif is articulated in a way that is distinctive to the concerns of the Samuel story.

3. For quite some time, scholars have been divided over the interpretation of "Hannah's portion," whether this is a "single" or "double" portion. Important in this sequence is the fact that Elkanah has two wives, clearly foregrounded as rivals, since one is childless while the other has children. This rivalry is very important, because Hannah's "portion"—whether a single or

16

double—clearly must be considered in this context of antagonism between the wives. It is in this setting that the sacrificial meal is distributed. The scholarly controversy is nicely summed up by comparing two translations, the RSV and its successor, the NRSV:

> On the day when Elkanah sacrificed, he would give portions to Peninnah his wife and to all her sons and daughters; and, although he loved Hannah, he would give Hannah <u>only one portion</u>, because the LORD had closed her womb. (1 Sam 1: 4-5, RSV)

> On the day when Elkanah sacrificed, he would give portions to his wife Peninnah and to all her sons and daughters; but to Hannah he gave <u>a double portion</u>, because he loved her, though the LORD had closed her womb. (1 Sam 1: 4-5, NRSV)

What are the various literary implications of the RSV and NRSV renderings? Does it make better sense for Hannah to receive a single or a double portion? It is possible that this scene reflects Elkanah's dilemma: even though Hannah is his favored wife, he can only distribute *but a single portion* to Hannah, because she has no offspring, and thus her ill-fated position is underscored: she cannot participate in the genealogical notice which commences the chapter. But once her womb is opened, she is able to contribute. Thus the "single portion" is deeply symbolic of her hopeless state as the book opens! Moreover, the single portion underscores Peninnah's (albeit temporary) triumph over *her* "rival" Hannah. Does the idea of a "single portion" make better sense in light of the overall narrative, and Hannah's transition from despair to exultation? One could argue that the single portion gives a "culinary" resonance to Hannah's helpless estate at the outset of the chapter. Consequently when she brings young Samuel to Shiloh at the end of the chapter, she brings all the ingredients for a feast. The two "sacrificial meals" thus illustrate her movement from dejection to delight.

4. How should Elkanah's words (especially, "Aren't I better than ten sons for you?") be heard? Is it possible that Elkanah, who is both "a father and a son" as Barbara Green observes, cannot relate to Hannah's desire, or is there something else going on here at a deeper level? Several commentators have suggested that this opening chapter functions as an overture to 1 Samuel as a whole. Robert Polzin argues that chapter 1 unfolds an elaborate parable, where the birth of a son provides implicit commentary on the birth of kingship in Israel. Polzin (1993: 18) compares the beginning of 1 Samuel with other beginnings:

> Just as the beginning of Joshua gave us a preview of major themes to be worked out in that book, and as the beginning of the book of Judges was a synopsis of what was to come there, so also we may suspect that the story of Samuel's birth contains within its texture threads that extend throughout the life and death of Samuel, well into the lives of Saul and David, and beyond. In other words, the opening scene of Samuel's birth may be a prospective statement about the entire book, and the answers that the book itself provides— indeed the entire complex of Samuel/Kings—could be answers to a set of questions that begin to be voiced in chapter 1.

Thus, Polzin hears in Elkanah's words to Hannah a covert comment on kingship. After reading Polzin's analysis, a host of questions come to mind: Does Elkanah's feeling of "rejection" anticipate and somehow comment on divine rejection when Israel asks for a king? How does Hannah's request for a son parallel or differ from Israel's request for a king? How does the birth of Samuel foreshadow the birth of the monarchy in Israel? Why do the images of "sonship" permeate this narrative, and how is this connected to the introduction of "kingship" in Israel?

5. Hannah's prayer is notable for a number of reasons, not least because it contains the first mention of "LORD of hosts" by an individual, which adds an interesting thematic dimension to Hannah's speech both here and elsewhere. It appears as though her "vow" is a vow of "Nazirite" dedication. The background lies in Numbers 6: "The LORD said to Moses, 'Speak to the Israelites and say to them: If a man or woman wants to make a special vow, a vow of separation to the LORD as a Nazirite, he must abstain from wine and other fermented drink and must not drink vinegar made from wine or from other fermented drink ..." When Eli accuses Hannah of "drunkenness," do you notice the irony that several commentators have pointed out? While Eli is wrongly thinking and accusing Hannah of being drunk, the irony is that she has just been praying for a Nazirite offspring, who must *refrain* from such indulgences! As Lyle Eslinger (1985: 79) notes, "Eli is completely mistaken. As Hannah points out, her actions are not the manifestation of drinking spirits, but of pouring out her spirit; not of pouring into herself, but of out-pouring herself." Further, when Hannah implores Eli not to consider her a "daughter of Belial," there is another layer of irony in that Eli's sons will shortly be described as "sons of Belial." This expression is the equivalent of a swearword in English. Evaluate Eli's initial response and subsequent "blessing" of Hannah, and compare Alter's (1999: 5) comment:

> The central annunciation motif of the type-scene is purposely distorted. Since Hannah receives no direct response from God—she prays rather than inquires of an oracle—Eli

the priest should be playing the role of a man of God or divine intermediary. But at first he gets it all wrong, mistaking her silent prayer for drunken mumbling, and denouncing her in a poetic line (marked by semantic and rhythmic parallelism) of quasi-prophetic verse. When in verse 17 he accepts her protestation of innocent suffering, he piously prays or predicts—the Hebrew verb could be construed either way—that her petition will be granted, but he doesn't have a clue about the content of the petition. The uncomprehending Eli is thus virtually a parody of the annunciating figure of the conventional type-scene—an apt introduction to a story in which the claim to authority of the house of Eli will be rejected, and, ultimately, sacerdotal guidance will be displaced by prophetic guidance in the person of Samuel, who begins as a temple acolyte but then exercises a very different kind of leadership."

6. There is a small point to consider as Hannah departs from the sanctuary in a rather buoyant mood. The NRSV renders her departure as follows: "Then the woman went to her quarters, ate and <u>drank with her husband</u>, and her countenance was sad no longer."

I have rendered this line as, "Then the woman went on her way, <u>and she ate</u>, and her face was not as it had been again," preferring to follow the Hebrew text rather than (as NRSV) the expansion of the Greek Septuagint. The simpler "and she ate" illustrates two things. First, she clearly believes the "prophetic" word of the priest, and so she "eats" of the sacrificial meal. Second, the Hebrew text is pointedly saying that *she does not drink*, especially in light of Eli's accusations and her own vow for her "promised" child.

7. The birth of Samuel underscores a complex wordplay that

reverberates throughout the chapter: the wordplay on the verb "to ask" (שאל), which in Hebrew shares the same root as the name "Saul" (שאול). Saul's name, therefore, means "the one asked for." Peter Miscall (1986: 14) summarizes the issue as follows: "the Hebrew root *sha'al*, to ask, to dedicate, and to inquire, occurs nine times in the story—1 Sam. 1:17, 18, 20, 27-28 and 1 Sam. 2:20; each refers to Samuel as the one asked for or dedicated. It takes ingenuity to explain the play on *sha'al* as offering a legitimate etymology for the name Samuel (*shemu'el*). The association of *sha'al* with *sha'ul* is patent." J. P. Fokkelman, (1993: 51) also makes a useful remark here: "Shortly the root שאל (*sh'l*) is to become the most important key word in the whole section. This verb, i.e., 'to ask,' has the task of linking and contrasting, in an extraordinary fashion, the two most important people in 1 Sam. 1-12, the prophet Samuel and king Saul!" Of course, it is interesting that both Samuel and Saul are "asked for" at different times, and in different ways. Why does the writer intentionally seem to connect Samuel and Saul at this early moment? Does this indicate that their "destinies" will be closely intertwined, or does this linkage rather suggest that their personalities may be similar or clashing?

8. Related to the last point is Hannah's speech to Eli near the end of the chapter, and her use of the same root, "to ask" ("saul"). Commenting on Hannah's use of "ask" here, Lyle Eslinger (1985: 94) observes: "*sha'ul*" in 1:28 foreshadows the name Saul in 9:2, which, in turn, may contain a subtle hint about the type of monarchy to be given to Israel." See also Robert Alter's comment here (1999: 8), "The English here is forced to walk around an elegant pun in the Hebrew: in the *qal* conjugation, [שאל] means to ask or petition; in the *hiphil* conjugation the same root means to lend; and the passive form of the verb, [שאול], can mean either 'lent' or 'asked.'" Further, Alter notes, "She spells out the action of

21

petition and its precise fulfillment, insisting twice on the root [שאל], 'to ask.' The Hebrew is literally 'my asking that I asked of Him.'" Comment on the literary and potential theological implications of the name "Saul" echoing throughout this opening chapter.

CHAPTER 2

The House that Eli Built

Then Hannah prayed, and she said,

"My heart celebrates in the LORD,
    My strength soars through the LORD.
My mouth grows wide over my enemies,
    for I rejoice in your salvation.
There is no one holy like the LORD, .
    there is none other than you,
        and there is no rock like our God.
You can no longer be multiplying your words,
    O Tall one! O Tall one!,
    or arrogance march out of your mouths,
For the LORD is a God who knows,
    by him wanton words are weighed.
The bows of the warriors are shattered,
    but the stumblers are armed with power.
The full are hired out for food,
    but the hungry cease,
Even the barren gives birth to seven,
    while the one with many sons withers.
The LORD puts to death and brings to life,
    sends down to Sheol and brings back up.

23

The LORD makes poor, and makes rich,
    brings low, but even makes to soar.
He raises the poor from the dust,
    from the refuse-pile he elevates the needy,
       to be seated with the princes,
          that they may inherit a throne of glory;
    For the pillars of the earth belong to the LORD,
       and on them he has placed the world.
He is guarding the feet of his faithful,
    but criminals are silenced in darkness,
    For it is not by strength that a man becomes mighty.
The LORD! The ones who rail against him will be shattered,
    against them from the heavens he will thunder,
The LORD will judge the ends of the earth,
    but will give strength to his king,
    and will elevate the horn of his anointed one.

And Elkanah went to his house at Ramah, but the lad was serving the LORD in the presence of Eli the priest.

But the sons of Eli were "sons of Belial"; they did not know the LORD. Now this was the custom of the priests with the people: when anyone offered a sacrifice, the priest's retainer would come along when the meat was boiling with the three-toothed fork in his hand which he would thrust into the basin, kettle, caldron, or pot—and all that the fork brought up, the priest would take away on it. So they would do to all the Israelites who came there, in Shiloh. Also, before the fat was burned off, the priest's retainer would come along and say to whoever was sacrificing, "Give the meat to the priest for roasting, for he won't accept boiled meat from you, only uncooked." And the man said to him, "Let them burn off the fat first, then you may take whatever you desire." But he said, "No! Give it now! Or if not, I'll take it with violence." The sin of the young lads was very

24

great before the LORD, for the men treated the LORD's offering with contempt.

But Samuel was serving in the LORD's presence, a lad outfitted in a linen ephod. And a little robe his mother would make for him, and she brought it up to him year by year, when her husband would go up to offer the yearly sacrifice. And Eli would bless Elkanah and his wife, and would say, "May the LORD provide offspring for you from this woman in place of what she asked for, who is loaned to the LORD." And they went to their place. Indeed, the LORD visited Hannah, and she conceived, and gave birth to three sons and two daughters—and the lad Samuel grew up with the LORD.

But Eli was very old, and he was hearing about everything that his sons were doing to all Israel, and how they were sleeping with the women who were hostesses at the door of the tent of meeting. And he said to them, "Why are you doing these things, which I'm hearing—*your evil things*—from all these people? No, my sons, not good is the report which I'm hearing, passing over the LORD's people. If a man should sin against another man, God can intervene for him. But if a man sins against the LORD, who can intervene for him?" But they would not listen to the voice of their father, for the LORD delighted to put them to death.

But the lad Samuel continued to grow up, favorably, with the LORD and with people.

And a man of God came to Eli, and said to him, "Thus says the LORD: 'Did I not clearly reveal myself to the house of your father when they were in Egypt, in the house of Pharaoh, and chose him from all the tribes of Israel to be my priest—to go up to my altar, to burn incense, to lift up the ephod—and I gave to the house of your father all the fire offerings of the Israelites? Why are you kicking at my sacrifice and offering which I have commanded as a refuge, and honoring your sons more than me by fattening yourselves with the finest of every offering of Israel, my people?' Therefore the LORD God of Israel declares, 'I indeed said that your house and the house of your father would walk before me always; but now,' declares the LORD, 'far be it from me! For those who honor me, I will honor. But those who despise me will be treated lightly. Behold, the days are coming when I will chop off your arm and the arm of your father's house—no old man will there be in your house. And you will stare with a distressed eye on all which is good in Israel; and there will not be an old man in your house ever again. But a man I will not cut off for you from my altar, so that your eyes will fail and your soul grieve, and all the increase of your house will die as men. And this will be a sign for you, which will come upon your two sons, Hophni and Phinehas: on one day, the two of them will die. And I will establish for myself an assured priest; whatever is in my heart and soul, he will do. I will build for him an assured house that will walk before my anointed one always. And it will be that any who are leftover in your house will come to bow down to him for a payment of silver or a loaf of bread, and say, "Attach me, please, to one of the priestly offices, so as to eat a morsel of bread."'"

POINTS FOR REFLECTION:

1. Why does Hannah sing? What other "songs" does Hannah's song remind the reader of? Commenting on the verbs "celebrate" and "rejoice," Eslinger (1985: 103) notes that these two verbs "also appear elsewhere in parallel construction (Pss. 5.12; 9.3; 68.4). In all cases, the verbs describe the joyful response of humble worshippers of Yahweh, who exult in the strength of their God. Also associated with all occurrences are statements about the futility and wickedness of man's pride and efforts at self-help, whether done in defiance or ignorance of the deity." Note carefully that the

books of 1 & 2 Samuel include "songs" at key structural moments: there is a song near the beginning, near the middle, and near the end. What is the purpose of this kind of structural arrangement?

2. As the words of Hannah's song are considered, what themes in her song are seen elsewhere in 1 & 2 Samuel? Compare the following very fine quotations from various commentators:

Rosenberg (1987: 124): This exuberant psalm expresses the historical outlook both of biblical tradition in general and of Samuel in particular: YHWH is invoked as the God of surprise, bringing down the mighty, raising up the downtrodden; impoverishing the wealthy and enriching the pauper; bereaving the fertile and making barren the fruitful—always circumventing the trappings of human vanity and the complacency of the overcontented. The many turns of personal and familial fortune in the ensuing chapters are an elaboration of the compressed strophes of Hannah's song. Indeed, the ensuing narration makes clear that Hannah's triumph and Samuel's entry into priestly service coincide with the house of Eli's fall from divine favor.

Walter Brueggemann (1989: 18, 20): These verses provide specific cases of transformation worked by Yahweh's power to transform and willingness to intervene. Yahweh presides over all human actions and is not deterred by or overly impressed by human actions and human resistances . . . It is Yahweh's capacity in the face of human action that gives hope to the weak and the marginal. Yahweh's intervention changes the disproportion of power and potential in human transactions. Thus in war the mighty may not win and the feeble may be strong ... This judgment about war anticipates the triumphs of Israel to come, perhaps with particular reference to David's paradigmatic defeat of Goliath ...The God praised is the judge who will preside over all the earth and all powers in it (v. 10). As judge, Yahweh will not only pronounce judgments but will actively intervene to implement those judgments. Yahweh will distinguish between the "faithful ones" and the "wicked" (v. 9*a*). The faithful are those who trust God's promises, receive God's gifts, and keep vows to God—people like Hannah. The wicked are those who rely on their own strength—people like Peninnah or the Philistines. Against the judging, ruling power of Yahweh, arrogant human strength cannot prevail (v. 9*b*). No power, no social arrangement, no alternative claim to authority can withstand the power of Yahweh (cf. 1 Cor. 1:25)."

Robert Alter (1999: 11): "The language here ["to seat among princes"] might anticipate the monarchic flourish at the end of the poem. "Throne" [כסא] in the next line can mean either throne or chair. Robert Polzin has made an elaborate argument for seeing not only Hannah's prayer but all of the early chapters of I Samuel as a grand foreshadowing of the fate of the monarchy with the old and failing Eli, who will die falling off his chair or throne, as a stand-in for the Davidic kings."

J. P. Fokkelman (1993: 104-5): The key concept of might and power is the most important one and spreads out the widest-ranging network throughout the poem. But it does regularly merge into, and make use of, the high/low polarity. We find true strength both high (in horn, rock, and heaven) and low (in the foundations of creation). Fake strength is under the illusion that it is high (v. 3ab), but is broken and terrified (4a, 5d, 9b, 10a), sinks into darkness, and is struck

28

down by lightning (10bc). Weakness is not divided into true and false, but is helped to its feet with care and a steady hand (v. 4b, 5c, and especially v. 8).

In this way the song of Hannah emerges as a study in power. It is an exploration by means of the remarkable compactness lyrics are capable of, and it is poetical preparation for the problematics which are to be continually dealt with and illustrated from many angles in the narrative prose of the books of Samuel: might and its embodiment in the monarchy. The programmatic place and function of the song of Hannah also clearly come into the light by recognition that it has vital links with the other poems in Samuel, the most prominent of which are: David's lament for Saul and Jonathan, his great song of thanksgiving after his becoming an established king and his miniature concerning the true ruler.

3. What exactly is the "sin" of the young men with regard to the offering? What are we gradually learning about the sons of Eli? When considered in light of the references to the "anointed" and "king" in Hannah's song, could there be any implicit criticism of Eli's leadership here? Could this be an *intentionally ironic* indictment on the house of Eli? Does this anticipate the speech of the itinerant man of God at the end of the chapter? Further, there seems to be a deliberate contrast drawn between the sons of Eli and Samuel. What could the purpose of this be? Note also the contrastive wordplay on the verb "to be great": the sin of the lads is "great" (גדל), whereas Samuel will "grow (גדל)" before the LORD in 2:21. See Brueggemann (1989: 23): "The linguistic parallel seems to sharpen the contrast intentionally. Both Samuel and the sons of Eli are 'great.' Samuel is 'great' as a mature man of God, Eli's sons are 'great'

29

in sin."

4. Outline some of the other abuses of Eli's sons, and especially their adultery in the sanctuary of God. Note that Eli hears the report that his sons are lying down with the women "who were hostesses at the door of the tent of meeting." Fokkelman (1993: 128) observes a wordplay between "hostess" and the title "LORD of hosts." Assess his comment: "The choice of the word [hostess, צבאות] is incriminating as well because it engages in a play on words with the famous title 'Lord of Hosts' [יהוה צבאות] which was mentioned, a short while ago, for the first time in the Bible. The priests abuse, therefore, a veritable host of women who themselves only have a mind to serve God, being in his presence to this end. This is a sacrilege whose insolence is of outrageous proportions."

5. What is the significance of Hannah having more children? How many of Elkanah's children have names? Notice Hannah's "reluctance" to let go of Samuel in chapter 1, and her stalling for time, it would seem, and telling her husband that she will bring the boy to Shiloh when he is weaned. Compare those actions with her annual "robe-making" here in chapter 2. Evaluate Alter's (1999: 12) comment on Hannah making the little robe:

> This is a poignant instance of the expressive reticence of biblical narrative. We have been told nothing about Hannah's feelings as a mother after her separation from the child for whom she so fervently prayed. This minimal notation of Hannah's annual gesture of making a little cloak for the son she has "lent" to the LORD beautifully intimates the love she preserves for him. The garment, fashioned as a gift of maternal love, stands in contrast to the ephod, the acolyte's official

garb for his cultic office. Moreover, the robe (me'il) will continue to figure importantly in Samuel's life, and even in his afterlife, as we shall have occasion to see."

6. In two successive sentences there is a reference to Samuel's garment ("But Samuel was serving in the LORD's presence, a lad outfitted in a linen ephod. And a little robe his mother would make for him"). Does this juxtaposition of garments (priestly ephod, prophetic mantle) symbolize or prefigure his multiple offices? O. H. Prouser (1996: 27-37) notes that often in 1 & 2 Samuel, "clothes make the man," meaning "clothing" is found at a number of key moments in the narrative. The reader should keep in mind future occurrences of "clothing" in the careers of Samuel, Saul, and David.

7. Describe Eli's "discipline" of his sons. Is it convincing—how does it reflect on Eli as a father? Why is this "discipline" not heeded? Immediately following this failure to listen (or effectively rebuke), an itinerant "man of God" appears in the narrative. Who is this "man of God"? Why are further details *not* given as to his identity? Identify his particular criticisms of Eli, and Eli's sons, Hophni and Phinehas. Is it not moderately ironic that this rebuking man of God uses a rhetorical question, the same device that Eli *has just used* in his (ineffective) rebuke of his sons? Fokkelman (1993: 135) provides a helpful structure to the oracle, noting "a clear and simple chronological order":
- the antecedent past (with the former appointment)
- the past (of complacency)
- the present, in which God curses
- the near future (of judgment)
- the distant future (with the alternative)

8. Does the reader have any clues about the "assured" priest who

is predicted as arising later in the narrative? Some commentators have pointed to 1 Kings 2 as the ultimate fulfillment of this narrative strand. Moreover, the "morsel of bread" idea is something of a poetic justice for the sons "making themselves fat" at the expense of proper worship: a corrupt priesthood eventually results in a hungry priest. Fokkelman (1993: 151) notes the irony that the descendants of Eli's sons have to "beg for bread" as a crime and punishment scenario for their gluttony. This irony, he suggests, is embodied in the verb "attach" ("Attach me, please, to one of the priestly offices"). It is striking that the verb "attach" (s-ph-h-n, ספחני) forms an "anagram" of the two names, Hophni (h-ph-n, חפני) and Phinehas (ph-n-h-s, פינחס). If indeed these two sons do not utter *a single word* of direct speech in the narrative, it is surely ironic that their future descendants are quoted as using an anagram of their ancestors' name!

CHAPTER 3

SENSORY PERCEPTIONS

But the lad Samuel was serving the LORD before Eli. Now the word of the LORD was rare in those days; vision was not breaking forth. At that time, Eli was laying down in his place. His eyes were beginning to weaken, he was not able to see. Now the lamp of God was not yet extinguished, and Samuel was laying down, in the temple of the LORD, where the Ark of God was.

And the LORD called to Samuel, and he said, "I'm here." And he ran to Eli, and said, "I'm here, for you called to me." He said, "I didn't call. Return, lay down!" And he went, and lay down. The LORD continued, calling Samuel again. Samuel arose and went to Eli, and said, "I'm here, for you called to me." He said, "I didn't call you, my son. Return, lay down!"

Now Samuel did not yet know the LORD, and the word of the LORD had not yet been revealed to him. And the LORD continued calling Samuel a third time. He arose and went to Eli, and said, "I'm here, for you called me." Then Eli understood that the LORD was calling to the lad. Eli said to Samuel, "Go, lay down, and if it should happen that he calls to you, then you should say, 'Speak, LORD, for your servant is hearing.'" So Samuel went and lay down in his place.

And the LORD came, and was standing, and called as previously, "Samuel! Samuel!" And Samuel said, "Speak, for your servant is hearing." The LORD said to Samuel, "Behold I am about to do something in Israel which will make the two ears of anyone who hears it tingle. On that day I will establish against Eli all which I spoke to his house, beginning to end. For I've reported to him that I'm about to judge his house forever, on account of the iniquity that he knew of: that his sons were blaspheming, and he did not weaken them. Therefore I've sworn an oath concerning the house of Eli, that the iniquity of Eli's house will not ever be atoned for by sacrifice or offering."

And Samuel lay down until the morning, and he opened the doors of the house of the LORD. But Samuel was afraid to report the vision to Eli. Then Eli called to Samuel, and said, "Samuel, my son." He said, "I'm here." He said, "What was the word that he spoke to you? Don't hide it from me! May God so do to you, and even more, if you hide one word from all of the matter of which he spoke to you." And Samuel reported to him all the words, and hid nothing from him. He said, "It's the LORD. What is good in his eyes, let him do."

Samuel grew up, and the LORD was with him, and did not let any of his words fall to the ground. All Israel from Dan to Beersheba knew that Samuel was assured as a prophet of the LORD. And the LORD continued to appear at Shiloh, for the LORD revealed himself to Samuel in Shiloh by the word of the LORD.

POINTS FOR REFLECTION:

1. This chapter provides the first of Samuel's "call narratives" (see also chapter 16), and in this episode the reader is privy to his transition from "lad" to "prophet." It is arresting that chapter 3 informs the reader that "the word of the LORD was rare in those

days," yet we have just witnessed a visit from "the man of God" at the end of chapter 2 immediately preceding. What is the point here? Is it a different *kind* of word in chapter 3? Or is the narrator being deliberately provocative, and subtly illustrating that mediating the divine word is more difficult than one may think?

2. What kind of atmosphere do the opening lines of this episode create in the reader's mind? Describe the ambiance that is invoked through references to Eli's incremental blindness and "the lamp of God." Does the rich "temple" symbolism serve to highlight the emphases in the chapter between blindness and insight, vision and perception? Further, reflect on the envelope structure of the chapter, and the symbolism of Samuel "opening the doors of the LORD's temple" near the end. Does this suggest (see Eslinger 1985: 153) the "restoration of God's word to Israel" and the "triumph of morning light over midnight darkness" in the land? Is there a connection, as Eslinger notes, between blindness and lack of vision bursting forth? "The scarcity of word or vision from Yahweh is a parallel, and perhaps even the logical result, on the physical plane of the blindness of Israel's priestly leader." Is Fokkelman (1993: 161) close to the mark when he notes: "Just as Eli has come to the frontier of pitch darkness, the temple is in danger of losing the light of God"? Does the presence of the young Samuel, actively involved in "opening the doors" of the sanctuary near the end of the chapter, represent hope for the future? Consider the following comments:

> Alter (1999: 16): Eli's blindness not only reflects his decrepi-
> tude but his incapacity for vision in the sense of the previ-
> ous verse. He is immersed in permanent darkness while the
> lad Samuel has God's lamp burning by his bedside. ... But
> the symbolic overtones of the image should not be

neglected: though the vision has become rare, God's lamp has not yet gone out, and the young ministrant will be the one to make it burn bright again.

Eslinger (1985: 148): In contrast to the atmosphere of darkness and unknowing in vv. 1f, symbolized by Eli's blindness and the scarcity of vision, v. 3 presents the hope of the future. The technique of foreshadowing a resolution to a present problem used in v. 3 has already been seen in 1.18. Here in v. 3, the insertion of the word *terem* in the sentence 'The lamp of God has not yet (*terem*) gone out,' indicates that, though the situation described in vv. 1f is gloomy, there is still hope. The flame is not yet completely extinguished.

3. What is the significance of the numerous times that Samuel "gets it wrong," and confuses the voice of God with the voice of humanity? Of course, the reader can excuse the lad, since "he does not yet know the LORD." However, on three occasions God calls to Samuel, and this must be a good time to get acquainted. Are there any portents for the future in this confusion? Furthermore, do you find it incredible that "the LORD was *standing*" right in front of Samuel? The same verb form is used in Exodus 34:5, "The LORD descended in the cloud and stood there with him as he called upon the name of the LORD." This clearly evokes a comparison between Moses and Samuel, although it is striking that Moses "calls" on the name of the LORD, whereas Samuel does not. What are the reasons for this hesitancy? Samuel requires the intervention of Eli, and the old blind priest is *indispensable* for Samuel "getting it right." As Fokkelman seems to note (1993: 163), there is a great irony in that Eli is "divinely used" in this sequence: "We cannot avoid recognizing that Eli's presence and insight are necessary for the

success of the plot. His mediation is indispensable to God who is attempting to reach Samuel with his revelation!" There is further irony in the fact that Eli is used to assist Samuel in hearing the "word of God" that is directed toward the doom of Eli's own house.

4. Notice carefully that Eli directs the young Samuel as follows: "Go, lay down, and if it should happen that he calls to you, then you should say, 'Speak, LORD, for your servant is hearing.'" Is this exactly what Samuel does? Again, carefully analyze Samuel's "obedience" to Eli's directive: "And Samuel said, 'Speak, for your servant is hearing.'" Commentators have noticed that there is a crucial omission in Samuel's statement: he omits the most sacred name in the Israelite vocabulary, "LORD." How serious is this "failure"? Consider Fokkelman's (1993: 171) summary:

> However, he [Samuel] leaves out one word, and that is the proper noun of God of all things. This is an eye-catching ellipsis which was probably valued as a theological subtlety by the writer's audience, with its literary grounding. Failure to utter the name fits in well with the information which was just provided: the laconic mention that "Samuel did not know Yahweh." It remains the exciting responsibility of the reader to decide in whose consciousness the discreet failure to utter the proper noun is to be situated. Is it Samuel who is shy or modest, or to a certain extent anxious, vis-à-vis the numen tremendum? Or is it primarily a message on the nar-rator-reader communication level?

How significant is it that Samuel omits the divine name, counter to Eli's instructions? To be sure, the excuse could be offered that he is young and does not know the LORD. Nonetheless, the fact

37

remains that "listening" and "obedience" (the same word in Hebrew) are major issues in 1 Samuel, and it is curious that these are among the exact reasons *Samuel himself* will declare to Saul why his kingship is rejected. Consequently, the reader should carefully assess this issue, and keep it in mind as the story unfolds.

5. Eli seems to sense that Samuel has been told something, and perhaps his own recent visitor (the itinerant man of God in the previous chapter) has set him on edge. Why then is he so keen to find out *exactly* what has been told Samuel? Further, how should a reader understand Eli's response, perhaps not even addressed to Samuel: "It's the LORD. What is good in his eyes, let him do." Is this a resignation? Repentance? Defiance? Who *is* Eli talking to here? Is he talking to himself? Note the irony: Eli earlier told his sons, "If a man should sin against another man, God can intervene for him. But if a man sins against the LORD, who can intervene for him?" Now, it seems, Samuel confirms that Eli has "sinned against God," and Eli realizes "who can pray for me?" Does Eli emerge as somewhat of a tragic figure? Compare Eslinger (1985: 151): "The narrator could have arranged his narrative so that Eli had no part in the success, but he did not. It is ironic that Eli should contribute to his successor's rise, but it is not a condemnation. If anything, Eli comes out of ch. 3 as a tragic figure ... Yahweh's mention of the location, 'in Israel,' of the thing he is going to do, and the statement that it will make all its auditors' ears buzz, seem to indicate an event of national significance."

6. As chapter 3 draws to a close, note the line: "the LORD was with him, and did not let any of his words fall to the ground." Whose "words" are being referred to here: Samuel's or the LORD's? What difference does it make? In conclusion, we have a dramatic "word" here disclosed to Samuel about the destruction of Eli's house and

the death of his two sons "in a single day"—hence the reader's interest is secured, wondering how on earth this word will be fulfilled. Evaluate Robert Polzin's (1993: 54) summary:

> Finally, not only does the account of God's revelation to Samuel end with a reference to the LORD's eyes (v. 18), it also begins with a reference to Eli's eyes, which had begun to grow dim [כהות]. In what way does this description of Eli's weakening sight stand for Israel's diminishing insight about kingship? If the parabolic prophecy of kingship's coming destruction is described as uttered at a time when "the lamp of God had not yet gone out," how may this matter of dimming insight have royal implications? What had Eli/Israel lost sight of? As D. N. Freedman has already suggested, the weakening [כהות] of Eli's sight in verse 2 may somehow be related to Eli's failure to "weaken [כהה]" his sons in verse 13. We can go further: the middle term connecting these two words is Eli's knowledge that "his sons were blaspheming God" (v. 13), so that Eli's weakening sight stands for his knowing failure to extinguish his sons' blaspheming. The theme of sons as stand-ins for kings continues in this chapter.

CHAPTER 4

ARK-EOLOGY

The word of Samuel was for all Israel. And Israel went forth to meet the Philistines for war: they set up camp in Ebenezer, while the Philistines set up camp in Aphek. Then the Philistines arranged themselves in battle formation, and prepared to meet Israel. The war itself soon unleashed, and Israel was hammered by the Philistines, who struck their battle lines in the open fields: the body count was about four thousand.

When the troops arrived back at the camp, the elders of Israel said, "Why has the LORD hammered us today before the Philistines? Let's get for ourselves the Ark of the Covenant of the LORD from Shiloh! Let it come into our midst, and it will rescue us from the grip of our enemies!" So the troops sent word to Shiloh, and from there they carried away the Ark of the Covenant of the LORD of Hosts, Who is Seated among The Mighty Angels. (Now the two sons of Eli were there with the Ark of God, Hophni and Phinehas.)

It came to pass when the Ark of the Covenant of the LORD arrived in the camp, that all Israel erupted in a huge battle roar, such that the earth itself trembled. And the Philistines heard the sound of the battle roar, and they said, "What's the reason for this great sound of the battle roar in the camp of the Hebrews?" Then they knew that the Ark of the LORD had arrived in the camp. The Philistines were terrified, for it was said, "A god has arrived at the camp!" They said, "We're doomed! Nothing like this has ever happened before! We're finished! Who can possibly save us from the hand of these mighty gods? These are the gods who struck the Egyptians with all kinds of wounds in the wilderness—You've simply *got* to be strong and be men, O Philistines, lest you become slaves of the Hebrews just as they have been slaves for you! So be men, and fight!"

Then the Philistines engaged in combat, and Israel was routed, with any survivor heading for home. There was a great pounding, with thirty thousand Israelite foot soldiers falling. Moreover, the Ark of God was captured, and the two sons of Eli—Hophni and Phinehas—died.

On that day a man from Benjamin ran from the battle lines, and arrived in Shiloh with his clothes ripped and with dirt on his head. As he entered, behold, there was Eli, sitting on his throne, at the side of the road, anxiously peering, for his heart was trembling over the Ark of God. Then the man arrived to report in the city, and all the city cried out. Eli heard the sound of the outcry, and said, "What's the meaning of this commotion?" Then the man hurried and came to Eli to give his report. (Now Eli was ninety-eight years of age. His eyes were standing still; he was unable to see.) The man said to Eli, "I'm the one arrived from the battlefield—just today I've fled from the combat zone!" He said, "What's the word, my son?" The man bringing the news answered, "Israel has fled before the Philistines, and there's been a great slaughter among the troops. Also, your two sons are dead—Hophni and Phinehas—and the Ark of God has been captured." Then, just as he mentioned the Ark of God, Eli fell off his throne backwards, beside the city gate. He had a broken neck, and he died, for he was a very old man, and heavy. He had judged Israel for forty years.

Now his daughter-in-law, the wife of Phinehas, was pregnant and about to give birth. When she heard the report that the Ark of God had been captured, and that her father-in-law had died (along with her husband), she doubled-over to give birth, for her labor pains

41

threw her into a convulsion. As the time of her death drew near, the women standing over her said, "Don't be afraid, for you've given birth to a son!" But she did not respond, and did not even take the matter to heart. She called the lad, "Where is Honor?," stating, "Honor is exiled from Israel" (concerning the capture of the Ark of God and her father-in-law and husband). She said, "Honor is exiled from Israel, for the Ark of God is captured!"

POINTS FOR REFLECTION:

1. Some translations attach the first line ("The word of Samuel extended throughout Israel") to the preceding chapter. However, understanding this sentence at the start of chapter 4 seems to make good sense: Samuel's "word" (that is, the word about the demise of the house of Eli), has national implications. And, of course, it is most fitting that the "word of Samuel" should frame the episode of the deaths of Eli, Hophni and Phinehas; after all, the opening chapters (as numerous commentators point out) delineate the theme of the "rise of Samuel" over and against the "fall of the house of Eli." However, Samuel himself will be notably absent for the next three chapters. Why is this?

2. The narrative of chapters 4-6 are often termed "the Ark narrative," since a main "character" in this stretch of episodes is the Ark itself. A number of scholars argued that this "Ark narrative" is a separate strand that was later incorporated into 1 Samuel. However, a host of more recent scholars have suggested otherwise, and these chapters are now seen as a vital aspect of the unfolding "plot of kingship" in the book of 1 Samuel as a whole. As you read through chapters 4-6, think about how the Ark narrative

contributes to the political idea of *kingship*, and the theological ideas about *covenant* and *divine sovereignty*.

3. Defeat in battle prompts "the elders of Israel" to call for the Ark. This is worth remembering because the next time the reader sees "the elders of Israel" in action they will be "asking for a king" in chapter 8. As the Ark is being transported to the camp of Israel, why does the narrator pause to provide an extended divine title ("the Ark of the Covenant of the LORD of Hosts, Who is Seated among The Mighty Angels")? Since this description appears to be for the benefit of the reader only, since no character is ostensibly involved, what is the significance of this description? Is there a hint in this passage that Israel is treating the Ark like something akin to a "lucky charm" or even an idol? In this narrative stretch where there is a palpable indictment of Philistine idolatry, could this be an arraignment of Israel as well? There is an interesting intertext in the book of Jeremiah, as Hamilton (2001: 224-25) remarks:

> This way of thinking [the Israelites are guilty of turning a symbol of God's presence into an idol] may suggest why centuries later, in his famous "Temple Sermon," Jeremiah drove home his point by referring to what had happened earlier to Shiloh: "Go now to my place that was in Shiloh ... I will do to the house that is called by my name ... just what I did to Shiloh" (Jer. 7:12, 14); "I will make this house like Shiloh" (Jer. 26:6). Compare also the reference to Shiloh's judgment in Ps. 78:60: "He abandoned his dwelling at Shiloh, the tent where he dwelt among mortals." ... It cannot be merely the fact of Shiloh's destruction that fuels the analogy between Jeremiah's Jerusalem and Samuel's Shiloh, for many other Israelite cities were destroyed. What provides the punch for the analogy is (1) Shiloh is the only other sanctuary we

43

know of that actually housed the ark; and (2) in both Shiloh and Jerusalem the people prostituted their relationship with God by trusting (falsely) in a symbol to save them. The ark did not save them; neither did the temple.

4. It is notable that throughout 1 Samuel the Philistines (who are superior from a technological standpoint) will be a persistent threat to Israel. Consequently, their characterization in this episode is important. How are the "culturally superior" Philistines presented? Also note that this chapter has a host of *wrong assumptions* in it, although the Israelites are certainly correct in stating that the LORD is responsible for their defeat in battle. However, their "solution" to bring the Ark is surely misguided, not least because of the stewardship of Hophni and Phinehas. Consider the theological assumptions of both Israel and the Philistines in light of the havoc that unfolds in this chapter, as Polzin (1993: 58) notes:

> The Philistines themselves are depicted as misguidedly igno-rant, a characterization that will make their coming victories especially hard to take for an Israelite reader. This almost playful picture of the Philistines preparing for battle on the basis of obvious misinformation is accomplished by the nar-rator's incorporating into the few words they speak (in vv. 7b-8) an unusual number of what Israelites would view as factual errors. "Woe to us for nothing like this has happened before!" (v. 7). If the Philistines mean that they have never faced Israel when the latter is accompanied by the ark of the covenant, perhaps this is so. But if they are suggesting that Israel never went into battle so accompanied, then as every Israelite knew—and the history we are reading has made abundantly clear—they are woefully in error. They say, "Who can deliver us from the power of *these mighty gods*?" (v. 8). How ignorant to believe that the Yahwists worshipped

many gods and that the ark of the LORD housed their presence! Finally, the Philistine belief that Israel's gods had "smote the Egyptians with every sort of plague *in the wilderness* (v. 8b) is another error that must have struck the Deuteronomist's reader with some force. We might even suggest that specific passages in the Deuteronomic History [Deuteronomy—2 Kings] are being playfully evoked here, such as Deuteronomy 11:4-5 or Joshua 24:5, in which statements about what the LORD did to Egypt are immediately followed by reference to the Israelites *in the wilderness*. The Israelite, knowing well such traditional depictions of the mighty acts of God, would have taken special pleasure in recognizing how the Philistines had misheard or misread their opponent's sacred traditions.

5. The description of an "anxiously peering" Eli is a rather ironic image, since the reader discovers moments later that the aged priest is *totally blind*! Speaking of blindness, the Hebrew phrase translated above as "his eyes were standing still" emphasizes the same verbal root used earlier by Elkanah, "may the LORD establish [i.e., cause to stand] his word." In this instance, Eli's "standing eyes" symbolize the fulfillment of the divine word *against him*. This underscores the "inclusio" or "envelope structure" to Eli's characterization: he is introduced in the narrative in the posture of sitting, and he departs from the narrative in a not dissimilar position, "sitting on his throne." Note his last portion of direct speech is "what is the *word* my son," and ironically the "word" is the fulfillment of the "prophetic word" spoken against Eli's house earlier in the narrative. The final notice of Eli's "weight" (he is described as "heavy," כבד) recalls his indictment by the man of God in chapter 2 ("honoring [כבד] your sons more than me"), and anticipates the lament of Eli's daughter-in-law, who mourns the loss of the Ark with these words:

45

"Honor (כבד) is exiled from Israel."

6. Incidentally, a brave translation of the messenger's report might be "the one bringing *good* news." Usually the verbal root is translated as "good news," as in Isaiah 52:7, "How beautiful on the mountains are the feet of those who bring *good news*." From Eli's perspective, the news is hardly good, but from the viewpoint of the average Israelite, the deaths of the corrupt Hophni and Phinehas cannot be all that bad. But Polzin (1993: 61) observes that this verbal root (בשר) almost invariably is used when news is brought that is *beneficial to the house of David*. When the report of this loss is considered from the perspective of David's house, is it "good news"?

7. The death of Eli's daughter-in-law in the final moments of this chapter provide a deeper meaning to the identity of the messenger at the midway point: "a man of Benjamin." What is the significance of the messenger being a "man of Benjamin"? Is there another "man of Benjamin" the reader will meet in 1 Samuel? Are there any other allusions to Benjamin's mother Rachel in 1 Samuel? Peter Miscall (1986: 29) hints that there is a connection between the birth of Benjamin in Genesis 35 and the birth of Ichabod here in 1 Samuel 4:

> Eli's death is framed by stories about his children—two sons and a daughter die, but a grandson, Ichabod, is born. Ichabod brings ambiguity with him, or, better, he adds to the ambiguity attached to the messenger from the battle lines, who is a man of Benjamin. Benjamin's birth is akin to Ichabod's, since his mother Rachel dies giving him birth (Gen. 35: 16-20). In Benjamin's case, there is an equivocation on his name and an attempted clarification. "As her life was departing (for she died), she called his name Ben-oni; but his father called his name Benjamin" (Gen. 35:18).

46

8. Why does the Ark "go into exile"? Is it because of, among other things, poor management and leadership by the house of Eli? This precise verbal root is used later in 2 Kings 25 to describe Israel being "exiled" to Babylon. Can this "exile" of the Ark prefigure the later exile to Babylon? Is there a message for the exiles here? Could it be that just as the Ark of the covenant was perfectly able to "survive" in exile, thus the "people of the covenant" can survive in exile? Are "the exiles" being directed to a new level of trust and dependence on God's sovereignty rather than their own devices?

CHAPTER 5

READERS OF THE LOST ARK

Meanwhile, the Philistines had captured the Ark of God, and brought it from Ebenezer to Ashdod. Then the Philistines took the Ark of God and transported it to the Temple of Dagon, where they installed it near Dagon. However, when the people of Ashdod rose early the next morning, look!, Dagon was falling on his face, on the ground, in front of the Ark of the LORD! So they grabbed Dagon, and restored him back to his station. However, when they rose early on the next morning, look!, Dagon was falling on his face, on the ground, in front of the Ark of the LORD! Moreover, Dagon's head and the two palms of his hands had been cut off, as far as the doorway—only Dagon himself was left! (For this reason, neither the priests of Dagon nor anyone entering the house of Dagon step on Dagon's doorway in Ashdod, even today.)

Now the hand of the LORD was heavy on the people of Ashdod, and he brought disaster on them: he inflicted them with painful hemorrhoids, both Ashdod itself and its vicinity. The inhabitants of Ashdod realized that this was the case, and said, "The Ark of God can't dwell with us, for his hand is severely against us, and Dagon our god." So they sent a message, and gathered together all the Philistine dictators, and said, "What should we do with the Ark of the God of Israel?" They replied, "Let the Ark of the God of Israel be redirected to Gath." And they redirected the Ark of the God of Israel.

But after the redirection, it turned out that the hand of the LORD was against the city, causing a great panic. He struck all the inhabitants of the city, from the smallest to the biggest, and hemorrhoids broke out among them. And they sent the Ark of God to Ekron, but when the Ark of God entered Ekron, the Ekronites cried out, saying, "They have redirected the Ark of the God of Israel toward us, to kill us and our people!" So they sent a message, and gathered together all the Philistine dictators, and said, "Send off the Ark of the God of Israel, that it may return to its station, and not kill us and our people," for there was a deadly panic throughout the city; very heavy was the hand of God there. But the inhabitants who did not die were struck with hemorrhoids, and the outcry of the city reached up to heaven.

POINTS FOR REFLECTION:

1. J. P. Fokkelman (1993: 252) notes that the events that take place at the beginning of chapter 5 are happening at the same time as the events at the end of chapter 4: "Whilst the soldier fleeing from the battlefield is returning to Shiloh, the victorious Philistines are conveying their most striking booty in triumph from the battlefield, which is ironically designated the Stone of Help, and are taking it to the city." Fokkelman further adds, "The suggestion which emanates from the analepsis is that their joyous entry into the city coincides with the arrival of the messenger in Shiloh. This synchronism accentuates the contrast between the two camps." Comment on this literary structure.

2. Furthermore, as chapter 5 begins there is a distinct note of Philistine triumph: they carry the Ark to a prestigious temple, and victoriously place the Ark not only as a trophy of their military

conquest, but also as a *religious* gesture indicating the supremacy of their god Dagon. Hence, the narrator highlights the degree of surprise through the Hebrew particle "look" that indicates the Philistine's visual perspective: a fallen and soon-to-be dismembered (with head amputated) Dagon! If, as Robert Alter notes, Dagon's name means "grain," then how else does this narrative go "against the grain" of Philistine expectation?

3. Lyle Eslinger (1985: 190) inquires as to what exactly is Dagon doing when he was "falling on his face" to the ground: bowing in defeat, or worshipping before the Ark? Further, Fokkelman (1993: 253) notes a similar posture of Goliath (another Philistine!) in chapter 17 ironically "falling down" before a representative of God who had just been mocked! It is striking that the Ark is not pictured as *doing* anything (that is, no struggle or recorded conflict)—only Dagon is involved in any activity. Why is it that this whole tableau takes place "at night"? Is this so there can be no accusations of "tampering"? From a theological angle, it is most intriguing that "Dagon" is continually mentioned, rather than "statue of Dagon" or "idol of Dagon." Fokkelman (1993: 254) reflects as follows:

> Although the descriptions of Dagon ...clearly deal with an image, nowhere does the writer use the phrase "the image of Dagon" in spite of the fact that he is quite capable of doing so. In this way he begrudges the Philistines the subtlety of a theological distinction between the *numen* himself and his effigy. As a consequence of his not allowing this graven image in his text, no bones whatever are made about the humiliation of the person of Dagon. It is really Dagon himself who is lying on his face before the God of Israel.

As far as the dismemberment and decapitation of Dagon, Fokkelman continues, "The statue is in pieces, as if Dagon is a

50

scoundrel whose extremities have been chopped off. The pieces which represent his hands have rolled as far as the threshold, and his head has come off." The reference to "Dagon's hands" provides a nice contrast, since Eslinger (1985: 193) points out that Dagon's "hands" are cut off, yet it is the "hand" of the LORD that is heavy against the Philistines! Are there any connections between the "fall of Eli" and the "fall of Dagon?" Is it coincidental that both sustain serious head injuries?

4. What exactly are these "tumors" that the Philistines are afflicted with? Ralph Klein (1983: 50) discusses this affliction in terms of the bubonic plague: "The name of this plague derives from the buboes or swellings with which the victim is afflicted. *CHAL* defines עפלים as boils or abscesses at the anus, or hesitantly, as buboes connected with the plague. Using the *Kethib/Qere* system, the Massoretes supplied the vowels for another word, טחרים (= *Kethib* in 6:11, 17), which has been related to an Aramaic word meaning 'strain at the stool.' This noun, consequently, is commonly translated as hemorrhoids." If Klein is right about the rather unpleasant "strain at the stool" ramifications, then it seems that the Ark is wreaking havoc in the deepest recesses of the Philistine anatomy. The King James Version captures the physiological dimension of their suffering: "the hand of the LORD was against the city with a very great destruction: and he smote the men of the city, both small and great, and they had emerods in their secret parts." How might an early audience have reacted to this description?

5. The strategy of the Philistine dictators is rather provincial to say the least. Why do they redirect the Ark elsewhere *in Philistine territory*? Are they reluctant to give up their war trophy and symbol of subjugation by returning it to Israel? Or does the mayor of one city simply pass on the problem? How does this characterize the

51

Philistine dictators? Finally, in view of the fact that there will be numerous allusions to the Exodus story in 1 Samuel 4-6, it is notable (see Eslinger 1985: 197) that the pattern of "those who escape one peril are smitten by another" is evident here, as a testimony to Philistine recalcitrance. Is this similar to Pharaoh's stubbornness in Exodus?

CHAPTER 6

RETURN OF THE KING

N ow the Ark of the LORD was in Philistine territory for seven months. The Philistines called for the priests and sorcerers, saying, "What should we do with the Ark of the LORD? Let us know what we should send it back to its station with." They responded, "If you're intent on sending away the Ark of the God of Israel, don't send it away empty, but by all means return it with compensation. Then you'll be healed, and it will become known to you why his hand hasn't turned away from you." They replied, "What compensation should we return with it?" They responded, "Since there are five Philistine dictators, five golden hemorrhoids and five golden mice, because one plague was on all of you and your dictators. So, make replicas of your hemorrhoids and your mice, which are destroying the land, and give honor to the God of Israel! Maybe he'll lighten his hand from upon you, your gods, and your land. Why harden your hearts like Egypt and Pharaoh hardened their heart? After he humiliated them, didn't they send them, and off they went? So now, take and prepare a new wagon with two dairy cows, who have never had a yoke lifted on them. Hitch the cows to the wagon, but take their young home, away from following them. Then take the Ark of the LORD and place it in the wagon, along with the articles of gold that you're returning with it as compensation placed in a box beside it. Then send it, so off it goes. Be watching: if it travels up the road to Beth Shemesh, its own

53

territory, then *it is indeed responsible* for this great evil done to us. But if not, then we'll know that his hand hasn't touched us, but it has simply happened by chance."

The people acted accordingly: they took two dairy cows and hitched them to the wagon, and restrained their *sons* in the house. They placed the Ark of the LORD onto the wagon, along with the box, the golden mice, and replicas of their hemorrhoids. And the cows went straight along the road, the road to Beth Shemesh; along one highway they walked, lowing as they went, and did not turn away to the right or left. The Philistine dictators were walking along behind them, right up to the border of Beth Shemesh.

Now as the people of Beth Shemesh were reaping the wheat harvest in the valley, they lifted up their eyes and saw the Ark, and rejoiced at the sight. As the wagon came to the field of Joshua of Beth Shemesh, there it stopped, and there was a great stone. They chopped up the wood of the wagon, and offered the cows as an offering to the LORD. Then the Levites brought down the Ark of the LORD and the box along with it, which contained all the gold, and placed it on the great stone. The inhabitants of Beth Shemesh offered sacrifices and presented offerings on that day to the LORD. The five Philistine dictators looked on, and returned to Ekron on that same day. Now these were the golden hemorrhoids which the Philistines returned as compensation to the LORD: one for Ashdod, one for Gaza, one for Ashkelon, one for Gath, one for Ekron—and the golden mice, corresponding to the number of all the Philistine cities belonging to the five dictators, from walled city to rural village. The great (meadow) stone where they rested the Ark of the LORD remains to this day in the field of Joshua, from Beth Shemesh. But he lashed out against the inhabitants of Beth Shemesh, because they looked into the Ark of the LORD. He struck 50,070 men, and the people mourned, for the LORD lashed out against them with a great striking.

The inhabitants of Beth Shemesh then said, "Who is able to stand before the LORD, this holy God? To whom will he go up, away from us?" They sent messengers to the residents of Kiriath-jearim, saying, "Philistines have returned the Ark of the LORD; come down and take it back up with you."

POINTS FOR REFLECTION:

1. The chronological notice "seven months" at the beginning of this chapter serves to illustrate that what is about to follow will recount the final days of the Ark's captivity before its eventual release, and to highlight the increasing Philistine anxiety. Moreover, Eslinger (1985: 203-4) notes that this chapter (in contrast to chapter 5), carries far more dialogue, providing "a realistic depiction of the distraught Philistines, who are anxious to relieve themselves of the ark."

2. For the first time in this narrative, "mice" are mentioned, although other ancient versions of this text (such as the Greek Septuagint) include references to mice early in the previous chapter. But assuming this is the first mention, what is the literary effect? Does it accurately portray the Philistine confusion? There is a subtle irony in that the priests of Israel, Eli and his sons, are accused of not sufficiently giving "honor" (כבד) to the LORD. The Philistine priests, in contrast warn their people, and suggest that they "honor (כבד) the LORD"! This leads to their further warning about "hardening" (כבד) their hearts, another allusion to the Exodus event, and further testimony about Israel's experience coming from Philistine mouths.

3. It is fascinating *where* and *how* the wagon is driven, and while no "driver" is mentioned, the reader surely suspects *who* it is that

maneuvers the wagon right next to a large stone in the field of "Joshua." Evaluate Eslinger's (1985: 214-5) comment on Joshua as a significant name in this context:

> The name of Joshua, the man in whose field the cart stops, recalls another more famous character who was chosen to lead Israel into the promised land when Moses was barred entry (cf. Num 20,12; Josh 1). Once again an allusion to the exodus story is used to indicate the significance of these events. In this particular example, the ark's passage onto Israelite soil in the field of a certain Joshua recalls Israel's own entry into the land under leadership of another Joshua. From the perspective of Israel's history, the return of the Ark into Joshua's field after the destruction of Israel's polity in ch. 4 would seem a perfect portent for the renewal of that self-same polity.

4. The Philistine theologians devise an elaborate plan to determine whether this painful affair has been caused by the LORD, or whether it has happened "by chance." Does their "test" of the LORD's hand seem designed to fail? After all, what are the "chances" of nursing mothers willingly abandoning their young and, without any experience, embracing a yoke and walking in a perfectly straight line? Evaluate the insightful analysis of Robert Alter (1999: 32-33), especially his comments about how "the cows went straight along the road, the road to Beth Shemesh; along one highway they walked, lowing as they went, and did not turn away to the right or left":

> This small but vivid detail is an even more striking exception to the stringent economy that governs biblical narrative. The last thing one would expect in a biblical story, where there is scant report of the gestures of the human actors, is a

specification of sounds made by draft animals. The point, however, is that the milch cows—more driven by the Ark than hauling it—are going strenuously against nature: their udders are full of milk for the calves they have been forced to leave behind, they mark with maternal lowing their distress over the journey they cannot resist. There is a peculiar resonance between this episode and Hannah's story in Chapter 1. There, too, a nursing mother does not want to be separated from her young, and, as we noted, special emphasis is placed on the physical acts of nursing and weaning. (The connection between the two episodes is underscored in the Hebrew, which literally calls the cows' young their "sons," not their calves.) In both stories, sacrifice is offered after mother and young are separated. Here, of course, the mothers become the objects of sacrifice; in Hannah's story, it is a bull, and, in symbolic rather than literal fashion, the son as well.

5. Describe the "transgression" of the people of Beth Shemesh. Is it harsh? What exactly is their curiosity? Where is "looking into" the Ark forbidden? On a numerical scale, does the number of casualties—50,070—seem rather large? Note the rendering of the NIV at this point: "But God struck down some of the men of Beth Shemesh, putting seventy of them to death because they had looked into the ark of the LORD. The people mourned because of the heavy blow the LORD had dealt them." The NIV circumvents the problem of the large number by surmising that "50,000" has accidentally slipped into the received Hebrew text. The problem, however, is that there is scant evidence for this on the basis of the ancient witnesses, and even the Greek Septuagint reads "and he struck down seventy men, and fifty thousand men." How would you respond to this text-critical issue of the "big number"?

6. It is notable that the inhabitants of Beth Shemesh call on another town to rid themselves of the Ark. Does this remind the reader of the very similar (perhaps deceptive) Philistine strategy of sending the Ark to another city? According to Joshua 9, Kiriath-jearim is a Gibeonite city, and the Gibeonites are famous for deception themselves! See also the comments of Lyle Eslinger (1985: 227): "The Bethshemeshites, aware that no one would take the ark if they knew the true story of its return, conceal the facts and make the description of the ark's return as matter of fact as possible. They say, 'the Philistines have returned Yahweh's ark,' failing to mention the peculiar manner of the ark's return. They are also deceptive in their instructions to the inhabitants of [Kiriath-jearim]. 'Come down and take up the ark to you.'" Further, Eslinger notes, "The Bethshemeshites conceal their real concern, that [Kiriath-jearim] take on the burden, in a geographical subterfuge." Evaluate the helpful summary of Hamilton (2001: 226-27):

> Accordingly, the Philistines are happy to rid themselves of the ark and they send it on to Kiriath-jearim (6:21-7:2). It should be obvious why the ark was not returned to Shiloh. After all, that is where it was to start with. Anything so explosive as to cause the death of thousands for viewing it is best kept out of populous urban areas and placed instead in "an out-of-the-way hamlet" (Eslinger 1985: 227). Additionally, as Eslinger points out, the messengers are careful not to tell the real story of why the residents of Kiriath-jearim should come and claim the ark: "The Philistines have returned the ark of the Lord" (6:21). They do not say, "Oh, by the way, we housed the ark for a while here, but fifty thousand of our citizens died for looking into it." Nor do

they say, "We want to get rid of Yahweh and the ark" (6:20; the Hebrew allows us to read "him" or "it"). What is offered as a privilege is really a subterfuge.

CHAPTER 7

BATTLE OF "HELP ROCK"

The inhabitants of Kiriath-jearim came, and took the Ark of the LORD back up with them. They brought it to the house of Abinadab on the hill, and they consecrated his son Eleazar to look after the Ark of the LORD. From that day onward, the Ark remained in Kiriath-jearim; the time lengthened, a total of twenty years. Meanwhile, all Israel mourned after the LORD.

And Samuel said to the entire house of Israel, "If you are returning to the LORD with all your heart, then expel the foreign gods and the Ashtorahs from your midst. Establish your heart toward the LORD and serve him alone, and he'll rescue you from the power of the Philistines." So the Israelites expelled the Baals and the Ashtorahs, and served the LORD alone.

And Samuel said, "Assemble all Israel at Mizpah, so I can pray to the LORD on your behalf." So they assembled at Mizpah, and drew water to pour out before the LORD, and fasted on that day. There they said, "We've sinned against the LORD." And Samuel judged the Israelites at Mizpah.

Now the Philistines heard that the Israelites were assembled at Mizpah. The Philistine dictators marched up against Israel. The Israelites heard of this, and were afraid of the Philistines. And the Israelites said to Samuel, "Don't stop crying out to the LORD our God on our behalf, that he may rescue us from the power of the Philistines." Then Samuel took a single young lamb, and sacrificed a whole burnt offering to the LORD. Samuel cried out to the LORD on

Israel's behalf, and the LORD answered him. Just as Samuel was offering the sacrifice, the Philistines drew near to engage in battle against Israel. But the LORD sent forth a clamorous thunder against the Philistines on that day, and threw them into confusion, so that they were hammered before Israel. The men of Israel went forth from Mizpah and pursued the Philistines, striking them all the way below Beth-Kar.

And Samuel took a single rock, which he set up between Mizpah and Shen. He named it "Ebenezer [Help Rock]," and said, "To this point, the LORD has helped us." And the Philistines were humbled, and no longer ventured into the territory of Israel. The hand of the LORD was against the Philistines throughout all the days of Samuel. Also, the cities which the Philistines had taken from Israel were returned (from Ekron to Gath), as Israel regained its territory from the clutch of the Philistines. And there was peace between Israel and the Amorites.

So Samuel judged Israel all the days of his life. Every year he would walk the circuit of Bethel, Gilgal and Mizpah, and he would judge Israel in all these places. Then he would return to Ramah (for his house was there), and there he judged Israel. And there he built an altar to the LORD.

POINTS FOR REFLECTION:

1. What is the significance of this chapter beginning with a chronological notice about the Ark? As Fokkelman (1993: 249) notes, "The period of time the ark in Kirjath-jearim gradually and stealthily lengthens into decades, and the reader would have almost forgotten it were it not for David who deliberately and solemnly leads it back into the light of history in II Sam. 6." Is this designed to interest the reader in the Ark's future?

2. Comment on the reemergence of Samuel after a lengthy narrative interval. One recalls that the last mention of Samuel is at the outset of chapter 4, where his "word was for all Israel," and now when he reappears he is "speaking" to all Israel. Consider these three questions:

a)   Does this chapter show Samuel at his best, as he "abruptly and decisively reappears"?

b)   Does this chapter portray the best of "theocracy"?

c)   Is this chapter designed to be a deliberate illustration of a (comparatively) better world for Israel on the eve of the monarchy?

3. Note that both the Philistines and the Israelites "hear," but have rather different responses. The Philistines "hear" that Israel has assembled at Mizpah, and respond aggressively, with their leaders ascending for battle. The Israelites "hear" and are terrified, although notably they lean on Samuel's spiritual leadership at this precise point. Eslinger (1985: 238) notes that there is a contrast between the beginning of chapter 4, when the Ark is called for in the midst of Philistine aggression, and here where the Israelites ask for prayer. Eslinger further cites H. W. Hertzberg, who points out that the verb "to cry out" is the same one used in Exodus, describing the Israelite helplessness because of "the hand of the Egyptians."

4. On a slightly different note, do the Philistines "hear" that Israel has gathered for a time of national repentance? That is, do they "sneakingly" (as Eslinger 1985: 240-42 describes it) choose a moment of religious import (when Israel is vulnerable) to attack? If so, then the divine thundering is even more enhanced, and the battle is over before it starts. Now, instead of running to their homes as previously, the Israelites run after the Philistines.

5. Speaking of reversals from chapter 4, reflect on the significance of naming the place of victory "Eben-ezer [Help Rock]" and comment on Samuel's speech: "In bringing us [back] to this place, the LORD has helped us." In other words, victory is totally credited to the LORD, as he transforms a place of failure into a place/point of triumph. This chapter also provides an opportunity to reflect on the role of the prophet: "Do not cease to cry to the LORD our God for us. . ." Consider Robert Polzin's (1993: 79) assessment: "the chapter describes a judgeship that is to be free from the dynastic impulse to which even Samuel himself will fall prey; 8:1-3 makes Samuel's attempt at establishing a dynasty like Eli's the occasion for Israel's disastrous request for a king. Judgeship based on the LORD's choice rather than judicial genes is the programmatic model of chapter 7." Does this prepare the reader for the climactic events of the next chapter, or provide a moment of sober warning?

CHAPTER 8

GRAMMAR OF DISSENT

It came about when Samuel was old that he assigned his sons as judges for Israel. The name of his firstborn son was Joel, and the name of his second son was Abijah; as judges, they were based in Beersheba. But his sons did *not* walk in his way: they turned aside after corruption. They took bribes, and distorted justice.

Then all the elders of Israel assembled together, and came to Samuel, at Ramah. They said to him, "Look, you're old, and your sons don't walk in your ways. So now, appoint a king for us, to judge us, just like all the other nations."

Now the thing was evil in the eyes of Samuel, because they said, "Give us a king, to judge us." And Samuel prayed to the LORD. The LORD said to Samuel, "Listen to the people's voice, to everything they've said to you. Indeed, its not you they have rejected; rather, it is *me* they have rejected from being king over them, just as they have consistently done—from the day I brought them out of Egypt until now. They have abandoned me and served other gods—now they're doing the same thing to you! So now, listen to their voice, only solemnly testify against them, and tell them about the judgment of the king who will reign over them."

And Samuel spoke all the words of the LORD to the people, the ones asking him for a king. He said, "This will be the judgment of the king who'll reign over you: he'll take your sons and appoint them to his chariots and horsemen, and they'll run before his chariots. Some he'll appoint for himself as unit captains of thousands and unit captains of fifties, others will plow his fields and gather his harvest, or make weapons for his war and accessories for his chariot. He'll take your daughters as aestheticians, cooks and bakers. He'll take the best of your fields, vineyards and olive gardens so he can give them to *his* servants, and ten percent of your seed and vineyard production he'll allocate for his officers and staff. He'll take your servants, your maids, your select chosen men, and your donkeys, and they will do his work. Ten percent of your flocks will be his, and you'll all be his slaves. And one day you *will* cry out because of the king whom you've chosen for yourselves, but on that day the LORD won't answer you."

The people, though, refused to listen to the voice of Samuel, and said, "No, it *will* be a king who is over us! Indeed, we'll be just like all the other nations: our king will judge us, leading us from the front when fighting all our battles.

Samuel listened to all the words of the people, and spoke them in the ears of the LORD. And the LORD said to Samuel, "Obey their voice, and cause a king to reign over them." Samuel said to the men of Israel, "Everyone go to their town."

POINTS FOR REFLECTION:

1. The father-son motif (as well as the pattern of "old leader" with sons) in leadership has been encountered so far in this book. The central example involves Eli and his sons, and the reader is well aware of the level of corruption perpetrated by Hophni and Phinehas. In chapter 8, no sooner is the reader informed that Samuel appoints his sons as judges, but we are told of their profiteering and dishonesty. Does this reflect negatively on Samuel as it surely does on Eli? Or is Samuel *not* responsible for the actions

of his sons? Victor Hamilton (2001: 231) wonders: why do the sons live 50 miles away from their father in Beersheba? Is this an effort by Samuel to "distance himself" from his sons? Does he know about their conduct prior to chapter 8?

2. The emphasis on "Samuel's sons" by the elders is important for at least two reasons. First, if Samuel was oblivious to his sons' corruption before, he is now informed. Second, the sons (as well as Samuel's age) become the "reason" for the request for a king by the elders. Speaking of the elders, the last time the "elders of Israel" speak is in chapter 4, where they call for the Ark to be brought onto the battlefield. Needless to say, that was a disastrous decision, and brought catastrophe to the nation. Does this "request" also have potentially disastrous implications? The reader also notes the verb "ask" (שאל), and how it forms a connection with the name "Saul" (שאול).

3. The request for a king "like all the other nations" is obviously important for the plot of this narrative—but what are some theological aspects of the request? Is it true that by requesting a king the elders (by extension) are rejecting God's kingship of Israel? How would an exile likely respond to this profound expression of "national *insecurity*"? Despite the desire for a king to lead them in battle, what is the true source of Israel's "national security"?

4. Why is this matter "evil in the eyes of Samuel"? Is he angry for "theological" reasons, that is, because the Israelites have rejected their true king, the LORD? Or he is angry for "personal" reasons, that is, because his own leadership is now rejected? When God speaks directly to Samuel and informs him, "Indeed, its not you they have rejected; rather, it is *me* they have rejected from being king over them," is God reminding Samuel who is really being rejected here?

Is this divine speech a rebuke of Samuel, or simply information?

5. Evaluate the divine opinion on the "asking" for a king. According to Eslinger (1985: 262), the LORD "has a much more profound understanding of both the nature of the people's request and the nature of Samuel's displeasure, in contrast to Samuel's clouded vision." Hamilton (2001: 232) provides a helpful summary:

> God's response to this [the people's request for a king] is most interesting. Not once but three times he instructs Samuel to "listen to the voice of people," adding to this on the third occasion "and set a king over them" (vv. 7, 9, 22). The judge and the prophet (i.e. Samuel) are the individuals par excellence to whom the people are to listen. Here, that is reversed. Samuel, the judge/prophet, is to listen to the people (Miscall 1986: 47). It is as if the writer is drawing a contrast between "a God who reveals his love in spite of being rejected" and "a judge who fails to conceal his selfish reluctance to become a maker of kings" (Polzin 1993: 88).

6. The issue of whether Samuel acts in a self-interested manner here is extremely important. Many readers of this text simply assume that the prophet is infallible, and only acts in accordance with the divine will at all times. But this assumption may merit some reevaluation in light of the complexity of 1 Samuel as a whole. Could there be a critique of the office of the prophet in this narrative stretch even as there is a careful consideration of the office of the king? Further, does Samuel follow the LORD's instructions *exactly* in telling the people "about the judgment of the king who will reign over them"? Eslinger (1985: 270-1) argues that Samuel's bias is evident in this speech: "Although one might infer that such stipulating and declaring are subsumed by the verb אמר in v.10, it

67

would seem that the peculiar usage of אמר with a definite object is specifically intended to highlight the difference between what Yahweh commanded and what Samuel did. ... Yahweh tells Samuel to *prescribe* 'the manner'; instead Samuel *describes* it. As a result of his misunderstanding of Yahweh's directive, Samuel proceeds with a lengthy description of what he perceives as the prospective disadvantages of the monarchy." Do you agree that Samuel is acting in a self-interested manner? Or is he acting in a way that is in complete harmony with the divine will on this issue?

7. The matter of Samuel's conduct in this chapter is a very important issue, because if Samuel's reliability as a character is problematic, it creates a tension in his character which will intensify as the narrative progresses. Evaluate the prophet's final actions in the chapter: "And the LORD said to Samuel, 'Obey their voice, and cause a king to reign over them.' Samuel said to the men of Israel, 'Everyone go to their town.'" Is the prophet stalling here? Why does he say "Everyone go home"? Robert Polzin is suspicious about Samuel's "inner motivation," since he has been directly commanded by God. How does the prophet emerge from this chapter? Evaluate Polzin's (1993: 87) further comments:

> The answer to these questions seems to lie in the area of con-
> trastive characterization. Given what God says in the chap-
> ter, his character zone with respect to Israel—as we have
> suggested above in chapter 1—is remarkably close in its
> emotive register to Elkanah's with respect to Hannah. The
> love of God for Israel comes across as predominantly disin-
> terested and remarkably magnanimous: "Oh Israel, am I not
> worth more to you than ten kings? Your desires here are so
> like your previous idolatrous deeds. Nevertheless, I will
> grant your request, only there will be limits set." On the

68

other hand, Samuel's words in verses 11-18 are full of self-interest, and this understanding of them corresponds both to the people's subsequent reaction and Samuel's own lack of action at the end of the chapter.

CHAPTER 9

WHERE IS THE HOUSE OF THE SEER?

Now there was a man from Benjamin whose name was Kish, the son of Abiel, the son of Zeror, the son of Becorath, the son of Aphiah, a Benjaminite. He was a man of wealth. Moreover, he had a son, and his name was Saul—an outstanding young man. There was no better Israelite than him: from his shoulders upward, he was taller than all the people.

It so happened that the donkeys which belonged to Kish, Saul's father, vanished. Kish said to his son, Saul, "Take one of the servant lads with you, and arise, go seek the donkeys." So he passed over the hill country of Ephraim, through the land of Shalishah, without finding. Then they passed over the land of Shaalim, but there was nothing. He then passed over the land of Benjamin, without finding.

As they entered the land of Zuph, Saul said to his servant lad with him, "Come, let's go back, in case my father ceases from the donkeys and worries about us." But he said to him, "Hey, listen, there's a man of God in this town. The man is honorable— everything he says really happens. Now, let's go there, perhaps he'll tell us the road we should travel." Saul said to his servant lad, "But how can we go? What can we bring the man? Surely the food from our provisions is consumed, and there isn't any present to bring to the man of God! What have we got?" The servant lad continued his response, and said, "Look! I've just found a quarter of a silver shekel in my hand! I'll give it to the man of God, and he'll tell us our road!" (Now, previously in Israel, if anyone was going to seek God, they would say, "Come, let us go to the seer," since what is now called the "prophet" used to be called the "seer.") So Saul said to his servant lad, "Good idea! Come on, let's go." And they went to the city where the man of God was.

Now just as they were going up the hill toward the city, they found some girls coming out to draw water, and they said to them, "Is the seer around here?" They answered them, and said, "Yes, he's right in front of you! Hurry! Now... umm ... Indeed, today he has arrived at the city, for today there's a sacrifice for the people at the high place. Just as you enter the city, you'll find him before he goes up to the high place to eat, for the people won't eat until he comes for *he* will bless the sacrifice after thus the invited ones will eat. So now, go up, indeed, him today you'll find him!"

So they went up to the city. Now just as they were entering the midst of the city, look, Samuel was coming out to meet them, en route to the high place. (Now the LORD had uncovered Samuel's ear the day before Saul arrived, saying, "About this time tomorrow I will send you a man from the land of Benjamin. You are to anoint him as leader over my people Israel, and he will save my people from the hand of the Philistines. Indeed, I have seen my people, and their cry of distress has reached me.") When Samuel saw Saul, the LORD spoke up, "Look, the man of whom I spoke to you! This one will restrain my people."

And Saul drew near to Samuel in the midst of the gate, and he said, "Tell me, please, where is this seer's house?" Samuel answered Saul, and said, "I'm the seer. Go up before me to the high place, for you're eating with me today. Then, I'll send you off in the morning, and everything that's in your heart I'll tell you. As for those donkeys lost three days ago, don't set your heart on them, as they've been found. For who is the object of all Israel's desire, if not you and the entire house of your father?" Saul answered, and said, "Aren't *I* from Benjamin? From the smallest tribe of Israel? From the tiniest of all the clans within Benjamin? Why would you speak to *me* like this?"

Samuel took Saul and his servant lad, and brought them to the private hall. He gave them a place at the head of those invited, approximately thirty guests. Then Samuel said to the cook, "Bring the portion that I gave you, of which I said to you, 'Set this aside with you.'" The cook carried in the special leg and all that was on it, and set it down in front of Saul. He said, "Look, that which has been reserved is now set before you. Eat, for it has been kept safe for you until this appointed hour, saying, 'I'll invite the people.'" And so Saul ate with Samuel on that day.

Then they came down from the high place to the city, and he spoke with Saul on the roof. They rose early in the morning, just as dawn was breaking, and Samuel called to Saul on the roof, saying, "Arise, so I can send you off." Saul arose, and the two of them, he and Samuel, went outside. As they were edging down toward the outskirts of the city, Samuel said to Saul, "Speak to your servant lad, so that he passes on ahead of us." He then passed ahead. "As for you, stand still now, so that I can cause you to hear God's word."

POINTS FOR REFLECTION:

1. There are some interesting similarities between the opening of chapter 9 and the opening of chapter 1. Victor Hamilton (2001: 233) points out that the introductions of Saul and Kish are similar to Samuel and Elkanah:

a) A similar phrasing in the first sentence of each chapter.

b) Four generations are provided in each genealogy.

c) The curious place-name "Zuph," otherwise unattested serves as a link.

d) The pattern of "sons" and "kings" alluded to in the opening chapter seems to be emphasized: "If Samuel is the answer to Hannah's request for a son, Saul is the answer to the people's request for a king."

At the very least, the reader is reminded that Samuel and Saul are inextricably linked, and there seems to be a deliberate narrative patterning to connect the "vocation" of the prophet in chapter 1 with the "vocation" of the king in chapter 9. Saul sets out on a journey to look for some lost donkeys, but what he finds is something rather different. He finds a prophet and new vocation for which he is wholly unprepared.

2. Note carefully the physical description of Saul, which is extremely important for the developing plot of 1 Samuel. Alter's comments (1999: 46) are worth considering: "Saul's looming size, together with his good looks, seems to be an outward token of his capacity for leadership, but as the story unfolds . . . his physical stature becomes associated with a basic human misperception of what constitutes fitness to command." Furthermore, this episode provides us with the first words of Saul, which as Alter describes (1999: 47), can provide an indispensable moment where the person's character is revealed:

> According to the general principle of biblical narrative that the first reported speech of a character is a defining moment of characterization, Saul's first utterance reveals him as a young man uncertain about pursuing his way, and quite concerned about his father. This concern, especially in light of the attention devoted to tense relations between fathers

and sons in the ensuing narrative, is touching, and suggests that the young Saul is a sensitive person—an attribute that will be woefully submerged by his experience of political power. But as this first dialogue unfolds, it is Saul's uncertainty that comes to the fore because at every step he has to be prodded and directed by his own servant.

3. An underrated character in this episode is Saul's unnamed servant lad. While a peripheral figure in the wider narrative, this intelligent young man has a very important role is this particular story. Consider the various words and actions of the servant lad (Hamilton, 2001: 234):

- In contrast to Saul (his employer), the servant lad appears knowledgeable about current events including the existence and locale of the "man of God."

- Without the decisive intervention of the servant lad, they would have returned "empty-handed," and certainly the story may have been different.

- The servant lad is decisive, whereas Saul is irresolute. The servant lad knows all about "the man of God" (in the previous chapter, we are told that "all Israel from Dan to Beersheba" know about Samuel, with the apparent exception of Saul). The servant lad's first words are confident, in contrast with Saul's first words, which are hesitant.

- The servant lad's small coin underscores the irony that Saul, the son of a "man of wealth," is flat broke!

4. Although it is difficult to capture in English, Saul's question to his servant lad, "What can we bring" (מה־נביא) are exactly the same

words as "What is a prophet" (מה־נביא). Polzin (1993: 93) notes that this is a key wordplay in a chapter that is as much about Samuel as it is about Saul. This is subtly emphasized through the narrator's "aside," reminding the audience that a "prophet" used to be called a "seer." Not only does this chapter answer the question "Who will be king?" but the role of the prophet is also subject to scrutiny. On a different note, it is ironic that Saul begins his quest for "divine" knowledge by seeking Samuel; later in his career, Saul (שאול) will be continually "asking" (שאל) for divine knowledge in a host of different ways.

5. Numerous commentators have pointed out that there is a "type-scene" in the chapter, specifically the type-scene of the "hero at the well" (compare Genesis 24, Genesis 29, and Exodus 3). The basic ingredients of this type-scene include the following: a potential hero is traveling away from home; he encounters a well of water (symbolizing fertility); a maiden or maidens are present; there is a conflict or questioning; followed by some domestic hospitality. In this episode, most of the requisite elements are apparent, but there is no "consummation" of the type-scene, leading commentators to suggest that this is an "aborted" type-scene that foreshadows Saul's "aborted" reign. On a deeper level, one could surmise that there is a comment here about Israel's "marriage" with kingship and their abandonment of "covenant relationship" with God due to the desire to "be like the other nations." Thus, Saul's failure becomes emblematic of a national failure. Incidentally, the maiden's speech in this chapter is translated quite literally, and at several places it really makes little sense. Gary Rendsburg (1999) has classified this kind of speech as "confused language as a deliberate literary device in biblical Hebrew narrative," meaning that the narrator is *intentionally* conveying the breathless rapidity of the maiden's words in the presence of this handsome traveler. If

indeed the maidens are speaking in a rather giddy and excited manner, does this add to the drama of the type-scene and intensify its "abortive" nature?

6. Note carefully Saul's first words to Samuel, "Where is the house of the seer?" There is obvious humor in that Saul does not realize he is confronting Samuel himself, but there are other layers to this unwitting question:

a) In the first instance, Saul seems to forget the maidens' words that the seer is a visitor to the town. The maidens do not instruct Saul to enter the town and ask directions to the seer's house. Why does Saul do this? Does this perhaps foreshadow Saul's "creativity" in following orders?

b) How would Samuel have heard this question, considering that "house" can also mean "dynasty"? It is slightly ironic in light of Samuel's previous "dynastic" ambitions in chapter 8, as he "appoints his sons as judges." It is ironic that the first king is asking the last judge, "where is the *dynasty* of the seer?"

c) Would this serve to explain Samuel's comment, "And on whom is all Israel's desire fixed, if not on you and on all *your* father's *house*?" Does Samuel say this with any hint of contempt?

d) This initial encounter between Saul and Samuel in many ways anticipates a relationship fraught with theological tension, misunderstanding, and perhaps even personality conflict.

7. It is significant that this episode features a sacrificial meal, since in Saul's penultimate narrative appearance of chapter 28, he will also partake of a ritual meal. The words of (presumably) the cook are obscure. Either there is a textual problem, or the cook's words simply do not make any sense to our context. In any case, Saul must feel rather overwhelmed as the guest of honor at a feast he was not expecting to attend. Would the odd words of the cook serve to *increase* his sense of agitation?

8. There seems to be a deliberate lingering on the "sunrise" on this first day of Saul's reign. On the one hand, it suggests a new day is dawning for Israel and indeed for Saul himself. On the other hand, it will provide something of a contrast to the later career of Saul, where so much activity seems to take place "at night."

9. As chapter 9 concludes, the reader may well wonder about the secrecy of Samuel, and his insistence that even the servant lad not be privy to the anointing. It is of course possible that Samuel may be trying to protect Saul. Some commentators, though, have wondered about Samuel's attempt at manipulation. Is he unsure about the selection (i.e. fitness) of Saul as king? Is he resentful? Or is this good pastoral practice. One thing is for sure: this level of intimacy will be short-lived, and never again be fully experienced between the "two of them."

CHAPTER 10

WITH THE PROPHET(S)

And Samuel took a flask of oil, poured it on his head, and kissed him. He said, "Has not the LORD anointed you over his inheritance as leader? When you walk away from me today, you'll find two men near the Tomb of Rachel at the border of Benjamin, by Zelzah. They'll say to you, 'We've found the donkeys that you went to look for, and hey, your father's forgotten about the donkeys and he's worried about you, thinking, "What should I do for my son?"' Then you'll step on from there a little further and arrive at the Oak Tree of Tabor, and there three men will find you, going up to God at Bethel. One will be carrying three young goats, another carrying three loaves of bread, and another carrying a wineskin. They'll ask you how you are, and give you two loaves of bread, which you'll take from their hand. After this you'll head to the Hill of God, where there's a Philistine outpost. When you arrive there at the town, you'll encounter a group of prophets coming down from the high place; there will be a harp, tambourine, bagpipe, and lyre, and they'll be prophesying. Then the Spirit of the LORD will rush upon you, and you'll prophesy with them, and you'll be turned into another man. Now, when these signs take place before you, do whatever you find at hand, for God is with you. Then you'll go down before me to Gilgal, and behold, I'll be coming down to you in order to present the offerings and sacrifice the peace offerings. You'll wait for seven days until I come to you, and I'll let you know what you should do."

As it happened, just as he turned his shoulder to depart from Samuel, God changed him with another heart, and all these signs arrived on that day. They set out from there to Gibeah, and look, a group of prophets to meet them! The Spirit of God rushed upon him, and he prophesied in their midst. Then, all who knew him in times past saw, and look, he was prophesying with the prophets! Each person said to the other, "What is this that's happened to the son of Kish? Is *even* Saul among the prophets?" Then a local man spoke up, and said, "But who is *their* father?" Hence, it became a popular saying, "Is *even* Saul among the prophets?"

He finished prophesying, and arrived at the high place. And Saul's uncle said to him and to his servant lad, "Where did you go?" He said, "To look for the donkeys. When we saw that they weren't around, we went to Samuel." Saul's uncle said, "Tell me, please, what did he say to you?" Saul said to his uncle, "He certainly told us that the donkeys had been found." (But concerning the matter of kingship, he did not tell him what Samuel had said to him.)

Then Samuel summoned the people to the LORD at Mizpah. He said to the Israelites, "Thus says the LORD God of Israel: 'I brought Israel up out of Egypt, and I rescued you from the power of Egypt and from the grip of all the kingdoms oppressing you. But today *you* have rejected your God—who saves you from your evils and torments—and you have said to him, 'Indeed, a king you *will* set over us!' So now, station yourselves before the LORD by tribe and unit."

So all the tribes of Israel drew near to Samuel, and the tribe of Benjamin was chosen by lot. Then the tribe of Benjamin drew near clan by clan, and the clan of Matri was chosen. Then Saul son of Kish was chosen. They looked for him, but he could not be found. So again they asked the LORD, "Has the man arrived here yet?" The LORD said, "Look, he is hidden amidst the equipment!" So they ran and took him from there, and stood him in the midst of the people. He was taller than all the people from his shoulders and upward. Then Samuel said to all the people, "Do you see the one the LORD has chosen? Indeed, there's none like him among all the people." And all the people gave a war-shout, and said, "May the king live!" Samuel then spoke to the people about the procedure of the kingship. He wrote it in a book, and set it down before the LORD. Then Samuel sent everyone back to their homes.

Saul also went home to Gibeah, but every valorous man, whom God had touched in the heart, went with him. But some "sons of Belial" said, "How can this guy save us?" They despised him, and brought him no gift. He remained silent.

POINTS FOR REFLECTION:

1. In the opening sentence of chapter 10, the NRSV follows the Greek Septuagint, and renders the text as follows:

> Samuel took a vial of oil and poured it on his head, and kissed him; he said, "The LORD has anointed you ruler over his people Israel. You shall reign over the people of the LORD and you will save them from the hand of their enemies all around. Now this shall be the sign to you that the LORD has anointed you ruler over his heritage: ..."

What is gained (or lost) through this "additional material"? Samuel certainly is more clear in the Greek version, but is this the purpose of the text? In view of the larger story, some have suggested that Samuel in fact may be trying to "overwhelm" Saul, and inundate him with prophetic authority. Do you agree?

2. Lyle Eslinger (1985: 322-3) notes that the "astonishing correspondences" between these signs and Saul's initial journey

toward the prophet (at the beginning of chapter 9) may confirm that indeed the LORD is with Saul. The reader should keep in mind the prophet's instruction, "go down before me to Gilgal, and behold, I'll be coming down to you in order to present the offerings and sacrifice the peace offerings," as this is a vital component in chapter 13. It seems that at some point in the future Saul is to go down to Gilgal. Samuel commands him to wait "seven days," and assures Saul that he will arrive to offer sacrifices. While it may be hard to believe, Saul's entire future as a king hangs on this one instruction!

3. Why does Samuel command Saul to join the prophetic group? A reader might expect Saul's first activity as "leader" to be something in the military sphere. Evidently, a key component of this scene is the response of people who have "previously known Saul." What do their words signify? Do they approve, disapprove, or is their reaction merely one of astonishment? Why does "Is *even* Saul among the prophets?" become a proverb (or perhaps a byword)? Why is the same "proverb" quoted in chapter 19?

4. Saul's inquisitive uncle is an interesting character: is he suspicious? If Saul has been anointed king, does the uncle have anything to gain? Is this uncle Ner, the father of Abner? Why would the narrator *not* provide the name of this uncle? On the other hand, why is Saul evasive? Would not the reader expect Saul to share such monumental news?

5. Why does Samuel assemble everyone at Mizpah? Has not Saul already been anointed? What is the purpose of this "lot casting"?

6. Saul is hiding among the suitcases: what does this communicate to us as readers? Is this humility, or willful

81

obstruction? Who (or what) is he hiding from: the office of kingship or the people of Israel? Could he be hiding from Samuel? Consider this appraisal of Lyle Eslinger, answering the question, "Why does Saul hide?":

> His action reveals, in a small way, a certain will for self-determination, and hence the potentiality for this meek and mild designate to frustrate Yahweh's designs. To hide when Yahweh has chosen him may be a futile act on Saul's part, but it does reveal a side of his character that becomes increasingly important later in his career (e.g. ch. 13).

Do you agree with all or part of this assessment? Is it curious that only the LORD knows where Saul is?

7. Note the same wordplay involving the verb "ask" (which also means "Saul")—first the people "ask" the LORD for a king in chapter 8, and then when the LORD provides one here in chapter 10, the people have to "ask" where he is hiding!

8. "Scoundrels" is literally "sons of Belial," an expression seen previously in 1 Samuel 2 (the sons of Eli, Hophni and Phinehas, are "sons of Belial"). Why do these scoundrels despise the new leader, and what do their words mean? Likewise, why is Saul silent in the face of their insults? Is he intimidated, or is he manifesting self-control? These fellows will recur in the next episode, so their rumors of discontent should be kept in mind.

CHAPTER 11

HISSING OF "THE SNAKE"

Then Nahash the Ammonite went up and camped in front of Jabesh-Gilead. All the men of Jabesh said to Nahash, "Cut a covenant with us, and we'll serve you." Nahash the Ammonite said to them, "By this I'll make the deal: everyone's right eye be gouged out! This way I'll put a disgrace on all Israel." The elders of Jabesh said, "Relent for seven days, so we can send messengers throughout the territory of Israel. If we don't have a deliverer, then we'll surrender to you."

The messengers then came to Gibeah, of Saul, and spoke these words in the hearing of the people. All the people lifted up their voice, and they wept. And behold, Saul came in from the field behind the oxen. Saul said, "What's with the people? Why are they weeping?" And the words of the men of Jabesh were recounted to him. The Spirit of God rushed upon Saul when he heard these words, and his wrath burned intensely. He took the pair of oxen and hacked them in pieces, which he sent throughout the territory of Israel by the hand of the messengers, saying, "Whoever doesn't march out after Saul and Samuel, this is what'll happen to his oxen!" And the dread of the LORD fell on all the people, and they marched out with one accord.

When he delegated them at Bezek, there were 300,000 Israelites, and 30,000 from Judah. They said to the messengers who had arrived, "This is what you'll say to people of Jabesh-Gilead:

'Tomorrow you'll have salvation, when the sun grows hot!'" So the messengers went and reported to the people of Jabesh-gilead.

Then the people of Jabesh said, "Tomorrow we'll surrender ouselves. You can do to us whatever is good in your eyes."

On the next day Saul arranged the troops into three divisions. They entered the camp during the end of the night watch, as morning was coming, and struck the Ammonites until the heat of the day. Any survivors scattered, and no two of them were left together.

Then the people said to Saul, "Who said 'Will Saul reign over us?' Give the men to us, and we'll kill them!" Saul said, "No one will die on this day, for today the LORD has brought salvation to Israel." Then Samuel said to the people, "Come, let's go to Gilgal, and renew the kingship there." And all the people went to Gilgal, and made Saul king before the LORD at Gilgal. There they sacrificed peace offerings before the LORD. And Saul greatly rejoiced there along with all the Israelites.

POINTS FOR REFLECTION:

1. The Qumran text of Samuel provides additional information on this scene. Robert Alter provides this summary:

> The Samuel scroll found in Cave IV at Qumran reports a general campaign by Nahash against trans-Jordanian Israelites. Here are the verses from the Qumran version (brackets indicate reconstructed letters or words, where there are gaps in the scroll): "[and Na]hash king of the Ammonites oppressed the Gadites and the Reubenites mightily, and gouged out the right eye of e[very] one of them and imposed fe[ar and terror] on [I]srael, and there remained not a man of the Israelites be[yond] the Jordan

84

[who]se right eye Nah[ash king of] the Ammonites did n[ot] [gou]ge out. Only seven thousand men [fled from] the Ammonites and came to [J]abesh-gilead. And after about a month"—the words that follow are identical with verse 1 in the Masoretic Text.

Some scholars refer to the Qumran introduction as "original," and argue that these verses somehow dropped out of the Hebrew text during the long process of scribal transmission. Other scholars are skeptical, and affirm that this introduction is "secondary," and provides more of a commentary and an expansion rather than the "original" text. In your view, what are advantages of this "supplementary" material? Or, should the concise and abrupt style of the received Hebrew text be retained?

2. The name "Nahash" means "the snake," which sounds like a rather intimidating name for a hostile foe. The origin of the Ammonite nation is recorded, rather ingloriously, in Genesis 19. From Nahash's "eye-gouging" reaction to the request for amnesty, what kind of overlord would he make for Jabesh-gilead if his invasion is successful? Facial disfigurement is a method, one guesses, of instilling fear into recently conquered subjects. Nahash's confidence is apparent as he agrees to giving them one week to find a "savior"; he is sure that no one in Israel will confront him.

3. It is curious that in the preceding chapter Saul is acclaimed as king of Israel. Yet in this scene, he is at home working his fields. To be sure, the angry reaction of Saul when he hears the news about Jabesh is in contrast to his earlier actions of "hiding in the suitcases" and "keeping silent" in immediately preceding chapter. The "rushing of the Spirit" is reminiscent of the "deliverer" in the book of Judges (and in fact there are a number of comparisons between

this episode and Judges 19). Note that Saul commands the people to march out "after Saul and Samuel"—does this suggest that Saul understands that "king and prophet" go together? What does this tell us about Saul? Does it imply that Saul is certainly willing to submit to prophetic authority? Does Samuel have the same understanding?

4. This episode presents Saul as an able military tactician. In light of the people's request (chapter 8) for a king to "lead them in battle," Saul is an instant success. The lightning military strike—at the morning watch when the Ammonites would be most vulnerable—certainly suggests Saul's logistical aptitude. It is striking that in an episode which is perhaps Saul's finest hour, the prophet Samuel is not pictured as involved. Where is Samuel during the majority of this scene? Why does the narrator not mention his involvement? Why does Samuel not have a more prominent role in this very important battle scene?

5. The final moments of the chapter provide a glimpse of Saul as a leader, especially in the fact that he gives the LORD credit for the victory, and in his words, "no one shall be put to death." What does this intimate about Saul, in this first action as king? Incidentally, what is the purpose of Samuel's "renewal" of the kingship? Did Samuel have his doubts about Saul, that have only now been resolved? Or would this kind of ceremony be normally expected? Some commentators have suggested that Samuel—otherwise absent from the chapter, although mentioned by Saul—is trying to "rain on Saul's parade." Is this a harsh criticism, or something worth pondering in light of Samuel's speech in the next chapter?

CHAPTER 12

VALEDICTORY ADDRESS, OR GRUMPY OLD MAN?

And Samuel said to all Israel, "Look, I have listened to your voice—to *everything* you've said to me—and I've caused a king to reign over you. So now, look, the king walks around before you. As for me, I'm old and gray, but my sons, they're here with you. I myself have walked before you from my youth until today. Look at me! Testify against me in the presence of the LORD and his anointed! Whose ox have I taken? Whose donkey have I taken? Who have I extorted, who have I oppressed, and from whose hand have I taken a bribe to cover my eyes? Then I'll return it to you!"

They said, "You haven't extorted, oppressed, or taken anything from anyone's hand." He said to them, "The LORD is a witness against you, and his anointed is a witness today, that you haven't found anything in my hand." They said, "A witness!"

And Samuel said to the people, "The LORD, who appointed Moses and Aaron, and who brought up your fathers from the land of Egypt! So now, stand still, and I'll judge you before the LORD, with all the righteous acts of the LORD that he did with you and your fathers. When Jacob entered Egypt, your fathers cried out to the LORD, and the LORD sent Moses and Aaron, and they brought out your fathers from Egypt and settled them in this place. They forgot the LORD their God, and he sold them into the hand of Sisera, general of the army of Hazor, and into the hand of the Philistines, and the king of Moab, and they fought against them. They cried out to the LORD, and said, 'We've sinned, for we've abandoned the LORD and served the Baals and the Ashtorahs—now then, rescue us from the hand of our enemies, and we'll serve you.' And the LORD sent Jerubaal, Bedan, Jephthah, and Samuel. He rescued you from the power of your enemies on every side, and you lived securely. But when you saw that Nahash the king of the Ammonites had come against you, then you said to me, 'No, but a king *will* reign over us,' even though the LORD your God was your king. So now, look, the king you've chosen, who you *asked* for! Indeed, the LORD has given you a king. If you'll fear the LORD and serve him, and listen to his voice and don't rebel against the mouth of the LORD, then even you and even the king who reigns over you can follow the LORD your God. But if you don't listen to the voice of the LORD and if you rebel against the mouth of the LORD, then the LORD's hand will be against you and against your fathers. So now, stand still and see this great thing that the LORD will do before your eyes: isn't it wheat harvest time? I'll call to the LORD, and he'll send thunder and rain. So know and see that you've done great evil in the eyes of the LORD by *asking* for a king for yourselves."

And Samuel called to the LORD, and the LORD sent lightning and rain on that day, and the people were greatly afraid of the LORD and Samuel. Then all the people said to Samuel, "Pray to the LORD on behalf of your servants to the LORD your God so that we won't die! Indeed, we've added to our sins the evil of asking for a king."

Samuel said to the people, "Don't be afraid. You've done all this evil, only don't turn aside from following the LORD, but serve the LORD with all your heart. So don't turn aside—especially after vanities, which have no profit and can't save, because they're vain! For the LORD will not abandon his people on account of his great name, indeed the LORD was willing to make you into a people for himself. As for me, far be it from me to sin against the LORD by failing to pray on your behalf. I'll teach you the way that's good and upright. However, you must fear the LORD and serve him in truth with all your heart, for look at all the great things he's done for you! But if you continue to act wickedly, even you and even your king will be swept away."

POINTS FOR REFLECTION:

1. In the absence of any temporal indicator, it would seem that chapter 12 follows immediately after chapter 11. It would seem that this is the "renewal of the kingship" that Samuel spoke of at the end of chapter 11. Describe the introduction to Samuel's address. Why does the prophet make reference to his sons? Have they not been discredited? Why are they "here with" the people at the outset of the chapter? Is this another chance to reject kingship, or a kingship renewal ceremony? David Gunn discusses "the sense of personal rejection" Samuel feels. What is your assessment of the prophet's tone and content as this speech commences? Indeed, is the this last occasion that Samuel speaks before "all Israel"? Is this his "farewell address"?

2. Compare the NRSV rendering of this portion of Samuel's speech:

> "And the LORD sent Jerubbaal and Barak, and Jephthah, and Samson, and rescued you out of the hand of your enemies on every side; and you lived in safety." (1 Sam 12:11)

Note especially the difference in the list of judges: the Hebrew text reads "Samuel," whereas the Greek text (followed by the NRSV) reads "Samson." Would Samuel refer *to himself* in the third-person (like a modern presidential candidate)? What difference does this make? Which do you think is the "original" reading?

3. Is there a slight contradiction here between the narrative report and Samuel's recasting? According to chapter 8, it is the corruption of Samuel's sons that precipitates the request for a king. However, according to Samuel it is the invasion of the Ammonites. Most commentators, regardless of their position, realize the incongruity between the events as recorded and Samuel's version of history in his oration. Consider Lyle Eslinger's opinion (1985: page 403):

> By avoiding the real reasons and occasion for the request, Samuel exposes his own sensitivity to it (cf. 8.6f). The discrepancy between the request as described in ch. 8 and ch. 12 is a relatively simple matter of a disparity between the way it was, and the way a deeply involved character would like everyone to believe it was.

What is your opinion on the reason for the tension between chapters 8 and 12?

4. The translation of this line—"if you rebel against the mouth of the LORD, then the LORD's hand will be against you and against your fathers"—is a literal rendering, but it has long befuddled commentators. Nonetheless, the literal sense is retained because, like other points of the speech, the syntax may be intentionally awkward to reflect the moment. As Samuel's discourse begins to draw to a close, how would you assess this speech? Hamilton (2001: page 243) notes that "Samuel uses, judiciously, a double quotation, one from an earlier generation (v. 10, quoting Judges 10:10), and one from the present generation (v. 12, quoting 8:19), the purpose of which is to glorify and put on a pedestal the earlier generation while condemning his own." How do you think Saul is

hearing this oration? Why is there no mention of the victory over Nahash "the snake"? Moreover, what about the issue of the "lightning and rain"? This is usually understood as a sign of divine approval for Samuel's speech (and the prophet certainly explains it as such), but are there any other options? Is this "the Perfect Storm," or a sign of divine *dis*approval?

5. Peter Miscall (1986: pages 72-3) notes that this speech is interpreted depending on how one ultimately views the character of Samuel. Consider his discussion of the "two poles" of the prophet:

> At one pole is the authoritative and stern prophet who declares his innocence and the people's guilt. They have requested a human king and have thereby rejected their true king, the Lord. Samuel's denunciation is severe but not unyielding. The people and their king will have a future— to be determined by their obedience to the Lord's word. This the "good" Samuel, the Lord's and the people's established prophet and leader. At the other pole is the authoritarian, harsh, and bitter leader who is forced to appoint his own replacement. He does it with resentment and acrimony. The people's request is evil, because it is a rejection of him. His denunciation of them is more personal polemic than divine word.

Is Miscall's reading of the "two poles" a useful way of understanding the character of Samuel? If so, which "pole" is more dominant in this speech of chapter 12? If not, how would you characterize the prophet's career?

CHAPTER 13

THE STRONG AND THE WEEK

Saul was—when he reigned, and reigned for—two years over Israel.

Saul chose for himself 3,000 soldiers from Israel. Saul had 2,000 of them with him at Micmash and the hill of Bethel, and the other 1,000 were with Jonathan at Gibeah of Benjamin. Saul sent the rest of the army home.

Then Jonathan struck the Philistine outpost at Gibeah. The Philistines heard about it, for Saul sounded the trumpet throughout the land, saying, "Let the Hebrews hear." And all Israel heard the report, "Saul has struck the Philistine outpost, and as well, Israel has become odious to the Philistines." And the army was called to arms after Saul at Gilgal.

Now the Philistines gathered to fight with Israel, bringing 30,000 chariots and 6,000 horsemen. Their army was vast, like sand on the seashore. They came up and camped at Micmash, on the east side of Beth Aven. Every man of Israel saw that they were in deep trouble, and their troops were hard pressed. And they hid themselves in caves, thornbushes, rock crags, tombs, and cisterns. Some Hebrews even crossed over the Jordan to the land of Gad and Gilead; as for Saul, he was *still* at Gilgal, with the army trembling behind him.

And he waited seven days, for the appointed time with Samuel, but Samuel did not come to Gilgal, and the army was scattering all around him. Saul said, "Bring me the sacrifice and peace offerings," and he offered the sacrifice. As it happened, just as he was finishing offering the sacrifice, look, Samuel was coming. Saul went out to meet him, to bless him. Samuel said, "What have you done?" Saul said, "When I saw that the army was scattering all around me, and you didn't come at the appointed time, and the Philistines were gathering at Micmash, I thought, 'Now the Philistines will come down to me at Gilgal, but I haven't entreated the LORD's favor.' I forced myself, and offered the sacrifice." Samuel said to Saul, "You've played the fool! You haven't kept the command of the LORD your God, that he commanded you. Otherwise, the LORD would have established your kingdom over Israel forever. But now, your kingdom will not be raised up. The LORD seeks for himself a man just like his heart; the LORD will appoint him as leader over his people, since you haven't kept what the LORD commanded you." Then Samuel arose and went up from Gilgal, to Gibeah of Benjamin. Saul counted the troops which remained with him: approximately 600 soldiers.

Saul, his son Jonathan, and the troops that stayed with them remained at Geba of Benjamin, while the Philistines camped at Micmash. Raiders marched out from the Philistine camp in three divisions. The first turned on the road to Ophrah, toward the land of Shual. Another turned down the road to Beth Horon, and the other toward the border road which overhangs the valley of Zeboim (toward the desert).

No metalworker could be found in the entire land of Israel, for the Philistines thought, "Lest the Hebrews make swords or spears for themselves." All Israel would have to go down to the Philistines if anyone wanted to sharpen a plowshare, hatchet, axe or sickle. The price was a *pim* for a plowshare or hatchet, a three-pronged fork or axe, or to straighten an ox-goad. Consequently, on the day of battle neither a sword nor a spear could be found in the hand of any soldier with Saul or Jonathan. Only Saul and his son Jonathan had them.

Then a Philistine garrison marched out to Micmash pass.

POINTS FOR REFLECTION:

1. The opening sentence of chapter 13 is notoriously problematic. Many scholars have suggested that words have dropped out in the process of transmission, and numerous suggestions have been made. The Hebrew text can literally be translated, "Saul was one year old when he became king, and reigned for two years over Israel," but this does not make a great deal of sense. Hence, suggestions such as the NIV have been made, "Saul was *thirty* years old when he became king, and he reigned over Israel *forty*-two years," inserting the numbers which may have dropped out. Ironically, this is a fitting textual corruption in a chapter that is so disastrous for Saul's reign, and sadly the truncated text acts as something of an overture to Saul's extremely brief tenure as king.

2. How is Saul's son Jonathan introduced? It may be something of a surprise that Saul is (presumably) married with a son old enough to be a military leader. Does the reader immediately think that Jonathan could be a potential successor? Since two fathers so far in the narrative—Eli and Samuel—have sired corrupt sons, Jonathan's progress should be carefully monitored.

3. Some have argued that the Philistine numbers can be translated as "3,000 chariots and 6,000 horses." At any rate, there is considerable Philistine advantage in terms of numbers, and the presence of "chariots" certainly points to an immense technological

superiority. In fact, the modern connotation of a "Philistine" as an uncouth barbarian is misleading here; throughout 1 Samuel the Philistines are consistently presented as having far better weaponry and logistical organization than Israel. In light of the military victory of chapter 11, evaluate the figure of Saul in the first part of this chapter. Does Saul look impressive, especially since he is standing tall with only a few troops against formidable odds?

4. Presumably the reason for "Gilgal" here in chapter 13 is connected with Samuel's instructions in chapter 10, and Saul's action of "waiting" appears to be specifically tied to Samuel's directive. Are preliminary actions of Saul in light of his troops hiding in holes and thornbushes positive? If not, how is Saul presented? Is the narrator sympathetic? The difficulty of this passage must surround "the offering." Saul seems to wait long enough—or does he? How does a reader understand Saul's explanation, "I forced myself, and offered the sacrifice" (or, "I felt compelled")? Is this a convincing explanation? In your opinion, is Saul defying the prophet's vocation, or acting out of desperation? Are military leaders elsewhere in the Bible commanded to "entreat God's favor" before a battle?

5. The timing of Samuel's arrival is incredible: *"just as Saul finishes with the offering, look, Samuel is coming!"* As John Calvin might say, this is probably the worst conceivable luck. Does Saul not wait long enough? If he does, then why does Samuel not come within the "appointed time"? Is Samuel delayed? Is he testing Saul? If so, is it fair? He calls Saul a fool—how should the reader understand this accusation? Consider Victor Hamilton's careful appraisal (2001: 245) of this interview between prophet and king:

Interestingly, in his rebuke (v. 13) Samuel does not say,

"Why did you not wait?" or "Why did you offer the sacrifice?" Nor does he say, "Why have you not kept the commandment I gave you?" (cf. 10:8). Rather, he says, "You have not kept the commandment of the Lord your God, which he commanded you." But in point of fact, it was Samuel who issued the command, not God, and God never speaks in ch. 13. One wonders if the only stipulation that Saul has broken is "Thou shalt not violate Samuel's authority" (Brueggemann 1990: 100), and thus that it is a "trumped-up charge to keep Saul on the defensive and under prophetic control (Polzin 1993: 129). For Samuel, it is not only "what God says, I say," but also, "What I say, God says," and although that can be empowering for one's ministry, it can also be lethally dangerous.

How would you respond to Hamilton's assessment? Furthermore, the issue of "dynasty" is intriguing—does this suggest that Saul *would* have founded a dynasty (if only he had not sacrificed / if only Samuel had arrived moments earlier)? This is surely ironic in light of Jonathan's favorable characterization thus far. Why does Saul not respond to Samuel's indictment?

6. Note how the episode concludes with some data about sharpening tools and the Philistine's corner on the market. What is a "pim" anyway? Some have suggested that this represents "two-thirds of a shekel." Note Peter Miscall's comment (1986: page 89):

The details of the description demonstrate an exact knowledge of the area of Philistine practice. The narrator knows what is happening not just in Israel but also in Philistia; he knows specific practices, not just generalities. Such knowledge reminds us that the lack of details, relevant information, etc., in other situations is deliberate and not the result of a gap in the narrator's knowledge. Any narrator who knows what the Philistines charged for sharpening plow-shares and axes should know whether Samuel and Saul are together at the same place and whether Saul wanted to respond to Samuel's denunciation.

The chapter ends on a suspended note about a forthcoming battle against the Philistines in which they are out-gunned severely. Any Israelite success will be wholly due to the LORD's intervention.

CHAPTER 14

BITTER AFTERTASTE OF HONEY

That day Jonathan son of Saul said to the servant lad carrying his weapons, "Come, let's cross over to the Philistine outpost on that other side." But he did not tell his father. Now Saul was sitting at the outskirts of Gibeah, under the pomegranate tree at Migron. The troops with him numbered approximately 600. Also, Ahijah (the son of Ahitub, the brother of Ichabod, son of Phinehas, son of Eli, priest of the LORD at Shiloh) was carrying an ephod. Now the troops did not know that Jonathan had left.

In the pass where Jonathan sought to cross over to the Philistine garrison there was a pillar of rock on one side, and a pillar of rock on the other side. One was named Bozez and the other was named Seneh. One pillar was situated north in front of Micmash, and the other situated south in front of Geba. Jonathan said to the servant lad carrying his weapons, "Come, let's cross over the garrision of this uncircumcised lot—perhaps the LORD will work for us. For there's nothing to hinder the LORD from saving, either with many or with a few!" His armor-carrier said to him, "Do everything in your heart! Take the lead; look, I'm with you 100 percent!" And Jonathan said, "All right, we'll cross over to those men and announce ourselves to them. If they say to us, 'Keep quiet until we reach you,' then we'll stay in our places and not go up to them. But if they say, 'Come on up to us,' then we'll go up, for God has given them into our hand, and this'll be a sign for us."

So the two of them announced themselves to the Philistine garrison, and the Philistines said, "Look, Hebrews are marching out of the holes where they've been hiding themselves." Then the men of the garrison answered Jonathan and his weapons-carrier, and they said, "Come on up to us and we'll let you know something!" Jonathan said to his weapons-carrier, "Follow me, for the LORD has given them into the hand of Israel." So Jonathan went up on his hand and knees, with his weapons-carrier following. They fell before Jonathan, and his weapons-carrier finished them off behind him. And in this first attack Jonathan and his weapons-carrier struck about 20 soldiers, in an area half the size of a plowed field.

There was trembling in the camp and in the field, and the entire army, the garrison, and the raiders, even they were all trembling, and the earth quaked, and there was a terror of God. And Saul's lookouts in Gibeah of Benjamin saw, and behold, the crowd was melting, and running aimlessly! Saul said to the troops who were with him, "Count up, and see who has left the troops." So they did a count, and look, Jonathan and his weapons-carrier were not there! And Saul said to Ahijah, "Bring the Ark of God!" (for on that day the Ark of God was with the Israelites). While Saul was speaking to the priest, the confusion in the Philistine camp was growing and multiplying, and Saul said to the priest, "Withdraw your hand." Then Saul assembled the troops that were with him and entered into the battle, but look, each soldier was striking his colleague with the sword, totally confused! As for the Hebrews who had been with the Philistines previously (who had gone up into the camp from behind), even they were now with Israel, Saul, and Jonathan. The LORD delivered Israel on that day, and the battle crossed over Beth Aven.

But the men of Israel were distressed on that day, as Saul had put the troops under oath, saying, "Cursed is the man who eats food before evening, and I am avenged of my enemies." So none of the troops even tasted food. The whole country entered the forest, and there was honey on the face of the ground; as the troops entered the forest, look, honey was oozing! But no one dared to reach his hand to his mouth, because the troops were afraid of the oath.

Jonathan, however, did not hear the oath with which his father bound the troops, and he stretched out the end of the staff which was in his hand, and dipped it in the honey from the honeycomb. As he returned his hand to his mouth, his eyes lit up. One of the soldiers then spoke up, and said, "Your father indeed bound the troops with an oath, saying, 'Cursed is the man who eats food today,' and the troops are exhausted." Jonathan said, "My father has troubled the country! See how my eyes lit up when I tasted a little of this honey! Imagine, if today the troops had eaten from the enemy's plunder that was seized, then wouldn't the strike against the Philistines have been greater?"

On that day they struck the Philistines from Micmash to Aijalon, and the troops were exhausted. So the troops wrapped themselves around the plunder, taking sheep, cattle, and calves, which they slaughtered on the ground. And the troops also ate the blood. It was reported to Saul, saying, "Hey, the troops are sinning against the LORD by eating the blood!" Saul said, "You're treacherous! Roll a great stone over to me now!" Then Saul said, "Disperse among the troops. Say to them, 'Everyone bring to me his bull or sheep and slaughter them on this, then eat. Don't sin against the LORD by eating the blood.'" So all the troops brought their oxen in their hands that night, and slaughtered them there. Then Saul built an altar to the LORD (it was the first time he had built an altar to the LORD).

And Saul said, "Let's go down after the Philistines by night and plunder them until the light of day, so that none of them are left." They said, "Do all that's good in your eyes." And the priest said, "Let us draw near to God here." So Saul *asked* the LORD, "Should I go down after the Philistines? Will you give them into the hand of Israel?" But there was no answer on that day. Saul said, "Come here, all you leaders of the troops, and find out and determine where this sin is today. For as the LORD lives—the one who has delivered Israel—even if it is with Jonathan my son, he will surely die." (But none of the troops spoke up.) Then he said to all Israel, "You be on this side, with Jonathan my son and I on this side." The troops said, "Do what is good in your eyes." And Saul said to the LORD, "O God of Israel, give perfection." Saul and Jonathan were chosen by lot, and the troops cleared out. Saul said, "Let it fall between me, and Jonathan my son." And Jonathan was chosen by lot. Saul said to Jonathan, "Report to me: what did you do?" Jonathan reported, and said, "I merely tasted—with the tip of the staff in my hand—a little of the honey. Behold, I'll die!" Saul said, "Thus may God do to me and then some, if you don't surely die Jonathan." Then the troops said to Saul, "Will Jonathan die, who worked a great deliverance in Israel? By no means! As the LORD lives, if even a hair from his head falls to the ground! For today he did this with God!" And the troops ransomed Jonathan, and he did not die. So Saul went up from following the Philistines, and the Philistines returned to their place.

Now when Saul had taken the kingship over Israel, he battled against all his surrounding enemies: against Moab, the Ammonites, Edom, the kings of Zoba, and the Philistines. Everywhere he turned, he did damage. He performed valiantly, and struck the Amalekites, and rescued Israel from the grip of their plunderers. These are Saul's sons: Jonathan, Ishvi, and Malchishua. These are the names of his two daughters: the firstborn, named Merab, and the younger, named Michal. Saul's wife was named Ahinoam, daughter of Ahimaaz. The name of the commander of the army was Abner, the son of Ner, Saul's uncle. Both Kish the father of Saul and Ner the father of Abner were sons of Abiel.

There were intense battles with the Philistines throughout Saul's life. So whenever Saul saw a warrior or a man of courage, he drafted him.

POINTS FOR REFLECTION:

1. Note the ambiance of the opening lines of this chapter, especially "Saul was sitting at the outskirts of Gibeah, under the pomegranate tree at Migron." Saul's posture of "sitting" will become increasing familiar as the narrative continues. Also note the presence of Ahijah the priest, and reflect on Peter Miscall's (1985: page 90) comment:

> An ominous note is sounded by the presence of Ahijah, a descendent of the cursed house of Eli. The judgment on the house contaminates Saul's house. Ahijah is the nephew of Ichabod, and the story of Saul is an excellent demonstration that "glory has departed from Israel." Ahijah is wearing an ephod, which is associated with inquiry of the Lord in the rest of 1 Samuel.

2. Evaluate the presentation of Jonathan as this episode unfolds. Comment on the tension between the heroism he displays, and the fact that (according to Samuel's denunciation of the previous chapter) he will never be king! Interestingly, when Jonathan sets out to attack the Philistine outpost, why does he "not tell his father"? Moreover, why is this chapter so long?

3. Jonathan's "weapon-carrier" emerges as quite an accessory. Is it possible that part of the reason for this servant lad's bravery is to illustrate the necessity of "loyalty"? If so, how does this reflect on the narrative from chapter 9 until now?

4. Clearly this chapter is crucial in the unfolding presentation of King Saul. How does Saul emerge from the various segments of this chapter? Note carefully Saul's interaction with his son Jonathan. How does their relationship fit with the other "father-son" relationships in 1 Samuel so far?

5. Why does Saul bind the army with "an oath"? Miscall (1986: 93) points out some connections between Saul and the Jephthah narrative in Judges:

> Saul, like Jephthah, crushed the Ammonites. Saul, like Jephthah, makes a hasty, stupid vow that threatens, and in Jephthah's case takes, the life of a child. Saul's oath, in some ways, makes even less sense than Jephthah's. At least Jephthah's vow was explicitly designed to ensure victory. The association of Saul's curse—"Cursed be the man who eats food before it is evening, and I am avenged on my enemies" (1 Sam. 14:24)—with victory is not obvious. Does he consider it a form of fasting? Is he convinced that some ritual is necessary? Saul's motivation for the vow is unclear. How serious is the error of the oath? Is this sin? Has Saul wittingly done what is evil in the eyes of the Lord? Or is Saul out of control—either harried by others or weak and unable to respond in a consistent manner?

Jonathan's statement "My father has *brought trouble on* the country" is ironic, since there is a reflex to the Achan narrative in Joshua 7, where Achan "*brings trouble*" on Israel because of his violation. The irony lies in the next chapter, where Saul (like Achan) will struggle with the objects "devoted to destruction" (according to Samuel's denunciation).

6. There is an interesting textual problem with the sentence: "And

Saul said to the LORD God of Israel, 'Give perfection'" (and "perfection" is only a guess). Compare the NRSV rendering of this sentence:

> Then Saul said, "O LORD God of Israel, why have you not answered your servant today? If this guilt is in me or in my son Jonathan, O LORD God of Israel, give Urim; but if this guilt is in your people Israel, give Thummim."

The NRSV is following the Greek Septuagint, which provides the longer reading. Again, the Greek translators may be attempting to resolve the same problem with the text we have, or they could be working from a more complete manuscript. At any rate, this episode highlights a tendency in Saul that will recur in the narrative: a virtual obsession with seeking the divine counsel. In your opinion, does Saul's increasingly erratic behavior in this chapter stem from the words of rejection in the previous narrative of chapter 13? Could it be that Saul is trying to "make up" for his "apparent fault" in the previous moment with the sacrifices? Once more, notice the wordplay on Saul's name, "to ask." Saul "asks" (or "inquires") of the LORD, but there is no answer. What does this imply?

7. The chapter concludes with a listing of Saul's family, and his considerable military accomplishments. If he has already "been rejected" from having a lasting dynasty, why does the narrator linger over these details? What is the literary impact of this very long chapter concluding on such a note?

CHAPTER 15

"TALKING 'BOUT MY (DE)GENERATION"

And Samuel said to Saul, "Me the LORD sent to anoint you as king over his people, over Israel. So now, listen to the voice of the words of the LORD. Thus says the LORD of Hosts: I am calling to account what Amalek did to Israel, what he put before him on the road while coming up out of Egypt. Now, go and strike Amalek. Devote all their property to destruction, and don't spare anything he has. Put to death man and woman, nursing baby and children, ox and sheep, camel and donkey." And Saul summoned the troops, and counted them at Telaim: 200,000 foot soldiers, plus 10,000 from the tribe of Judah.

Then Saul arrived at the city of Amalek, and set an ambush in a dry riverbed. Saul said to the Kenites, "Go! Take off! Get down from the midst of the Amalekites, lest I remove you along with him. For you showed loyalty with the Israelites when they were coming up out of Egypt." So the Kenites took off from the midst of Amalek. Then Saul struck Amalek from Havilah until you come to Shur, right to the border of Egypt.

And Saul summoned the troops, and counted them at Telaim: 200,000 foot soldiers, plus 10,000 from the tribe of Judah. He captured alive Agag, king of Amalek, but he devoted all the people to destruction with the edge of the sword. Saul and the people spared Agag, along with the best of the flocks, cattle, the second-born animals, the rams, and all that was good; this they were unwilling to devote to destruction. But if any property was despised or worthless, it was devoted to destruction.

Then the word of the LORD came to Samuel, saying, "I repent that I caused Saul to reign as king, for he has turned back from following me, and he hasn't raised up my words." This burned Samuel, and he cried out to the LORD all night. And Samuel arose early to meet Saul in the morning, and it was reported to Samuel, saying, "Saul has arrived at Carmel, and look, he is erecting a monument for himself, and he has turned, crossed over, and gone down to Gilgal."

And Samuel came to Saul, and Saul said to him, "May you be blessed by the LORD—I've raised up the word of the LORD!" Samuel said, "What is the sound of this flock in my ears? What is the voice of the cattle that I hear?" Saul said, "They've brought them from Amalek, for the troops spared the best flocks and cattle in order to sacrifice to the LORD your God. The rest we've devoted to destruction." Samuel said to Saul, "Drop it! Let me report to you what the LORD said to me last night." He said, "Speak." Samuel said, "Are you not, though once little in your own eyes, head of Israel's tribes? And the LORD anointed you as king over Israel. The LORD sent you on a journey, and said, 'Go, devote to destruction the sinners, Amalek. Fight against him until they're finished.' So why haven't you listened to the voice of the LORD? You flew down on the plunder, and you've done evil in the eyes of the LORD." And Saul said to Samuel, "Yet I did listen to the voice of the LORD, and I went on the journey that the LORD sent me on. I've brought Agag, king of Amalek, and Amalek I've devoted to destruction. The people took flocks, cattle, and second-born animals from the plunder that was devoted to destruction in order to sacrifice to the LORD your God at Gilgal."

Samuel said, "Is it a delight to the LORD if there are offerings and sacrifices when the issue is listening to the voice of the LORD? Look, listening is better than sacrifice, to be observant is better than the best portion of rams. Indeed, rebellion is like the sin of divination, and defiance is like the wickedness of teraphim. Because you've rejected the word of the LORD, he has rejected you as king."

And Saul said to Samuel, "I've sinned, for I've passed over the mouth of the LORD and your words. Indeed, I was afraid of the troops, and I listened to their voice. But now, forgive my sin and turn back with me that I may worship the LORD." Samuel said to Saul, "I won't turn back with you, for you've rejected the word of the LORD and he has rejected you from being king over Israel." And Samuel turned around to walk away, but Saul took hold of the wing of his robe, and it ripped. Samuel said to him, "The LORD has ripped the kingdom of Israel from you today! He has given it to your neighbor, one better than you. Moreover, the Eminence of Israel doesn't deal falsely and doesn't repent—for he's not a man that he would repent. He said, "I've sinned. Now, honor me, please, in front of the elders of the people and in front of Israel. Turn back with me, so I can worship the LORD your God." And Samuel turned back behind Saul, and Saul worshipped the LORD.

And Samuel said, "Bring me Agag, king of Amalek." Then Agag walked toward him securely, and Agag said, "Truly the bitterness of death has been turned aside!" Samuel said, "Just like your sword has created barren wives, so your mother's going to be a barren wife!" Then Samuel severed Agag before the LORD in Gilgal.

And Samuel departed for Ramah, while Saul went up to his house at Gibeah-Saul. Samuel did not see Saul again until the day of his death. Indeed, Samuel lamented over Saul, and the LORD repented that he had caused Saul to become king over Israel.

POINTS FOR REFLECTION:

1. It is notable that this chapter begins with a conflict (Israel vs. the Amalekites), because it is a story about conflict on a number of levels. There is the obvious conflict between Samuel and Saul, the LORD and Saul, and also, perhaps more subtly, a conflict between Samuel and the LORD. In the first instance, note carefully how Samuel frames the command to Saul. What does this tell the reader about Samuel's attitude toward Saul at this point? If Saul has already been rejected by Samuel, why is he being commissioned for this assignment? In the previous chapter, Saul attacks the Philistines, but why does Samuel not appear at all in chapter 14?

2. This episode presupposes the background of a discussion about the Amalekites in Deuteronomy, and the notion of "the ban," a difficult Hebrew term (חרם) that I have translated "devote to destruction." To "devote to destruction" takes place in the context of a "holy war," where everything possessed by the adversary is utterly destroyed. Consider the relevant passage in Deuteronomy 25:17-19:

> Remember what Amalek did to you on your journey out of Egypt, how he attacked you on the way, when you were faint and weary, and struck down all who lagged behind you; he did not fear God. Therefore when the LORD your God has given you rest from all your enemies on every hand, in the land that the LORD your God is giving you as an inheritance to possess, you shall blot out the remembrance of Amalek from under heaven; do not forget. (NRSV)

3. Both Saul's recruiting of troops for this campaign and the attack itself is successful, reminiscent of Saul's military success in chapter 11 against the Ammonites. However, Samuel did not

celebrate that victory, and a reader may guess that the same thing will happen here.

4. There are two details of Saul's actions that should pique the reader's interest. First, Saul warns "the Kenites" and invites them to leave the Amalekites lest they be consumed in the battle. It is curious that there is no allusion in the Torah as to when exactly the Kenites "showed loyalty with the Israelites when they were coming up out of Egypt." Does Saul's action toward the Kenites portray him as a compassionate king, or is this another example of Saul "going beyond" Samuel's instructions? Is there any connection here with Balaam's oracle in Numbers 24:20-21? Does Saul view himself as fulfilling various prophetic utterances? Second, what are some implications of Saul "sparing" the king and the best of the property? Does this go beyond (or even transgress) Samuel's instructions? Is Saul saving the king and best of the plunder for a sacrifice *because of* his earlier blunder with a sacrifice in chapter 13? At a minimum, does this "Kenite" vignette foreshadow Saul's claim to be "doing the right thing" in sparing the best of the Amalekite plunder for sacrifice?

5. The reader is provided with direct speech from God regarding King Saul, "I repent/regret (נחם) that I caused Saul to reign as king, for he has turned back from following me, and he has not raised up my words." The Hebrew term "repent/regret" (נחם) can literally be translated as "repent," although this raises theological problems for Christian interpreters. A close parallel would be Genesis 6. God is obviously not guilty of some sort of moral deviance, but this narrative is intentionally rather complicated. Further, this is an important issue, because later in the chapter Samuel will tell Saul that God "does not regret/repent" (נחם), yet both God and the narrator (in the final sentence of the chapter) affirm that God does

"regret/repent." This is potentially quite serious for the prophet, since he tells the king "God does not regret/repent," which is contradicted by both God and the narrator. Respond to the comments of Yairah Amit (2001: 100-01):

> How can Samuel state that God does not change his mind, when God told him directly and explicitly that he regretted making Saul king? (In the Hebrew, the same verb, nhm, is used in both statements).

> The reader, coming across these three statements, spoken by God, by the prophet, and by the narrator, must choose which of them to believe. Surely we must believe the word of God, which is matched by the narrator's statement, namely, that God does and did regret what he had done. But this raises the question, how reliable is the prophet who is God's emissary? Samuel proceeds to describe God in singular terms that emphasize the difference between Him and human beings—specifically that God does not change his mind, even though this contradicts the statements made by God himself and by the narrator. Moreover, deciding that the prophet is not to be trusted in this case can have wider implications. It may cast doubt not only about the particular case of Samuel's attitude to Saul, but also about statements made by prophets elsewhere in the Bible. As we go on reading, we find in 1 Kings 13:11-19 a prophet who lies in God's name.

> Returning to our story, we can only speculate about why Samuel deviated from God's word, and indeed there are any number of speculations in the commentaries on this passage. Possibly Samuel meant to say that God did not regret

110

his decision to remove the kingship from Saul, but being furious with Saul, he went on to say that unlike men, God did not change his mind, thus speaking his own mind rather than God's. The simple conclusion from this story is that even a prophet may not always be totally reliable. Such a conclusion accords with the world of biblical beliefs and views, which stresses the difference between the human and the divine. Human beings have failings and cannot be compared with the deity, which is why biblical stories are replete with sinful kings and even depict prophets who deviate from their mission. Readers of biblical stories must therefore keep reminding themselves that God and the narrator are always to be believed, whereas the speech of the characters in the story, even if they are God's emissaries, must be checked.

6. Commentators are divided over the reasons for Samuel's "burning anger" over God's "regret." Some scholars feel that Samuel has compassion for Saul, whereas other scholars believe that Samuel is angry because his own position is now potentially undermined. In your opinion, why is Samuel so angry?

7. The mention of Saul traveling to "Gilgal" is highly ironic, especially if (after erecting the monument) the purpose for Saul's trip to Gilgal is "to sacrifice" the best plunder of the Amalekites. Saul's sacrifice at Gilgal in chapter 13 results in Samuel's first denunciation, and Gilgal now becomes the *spatial setting* for Saul's second denunciation from Samuel. What do you think of Saul's "rationale" for sparing the best? Should he be given "the benefit of the doubt" here? Or is Saul categorically guilty of violating the prophet's instructions?

8. The quality of Samuel's condemnation is unequivocal. Does

Samuel's speech to Saul sound rehearsed, or is it extemporaneous based on the "bleating of the sheep" which he hears? Miscall (1986: page 111) asks: "Is this the stern, true prophet of the Lord declaring the Lord's word versus a sinner, or is this a stern, unrelenting prophet denouncing a rival?" Comment on Saul's reaction, explanation(s), and eventual request for forgiveness. Why does Saul want to worship, and why is he so insistent? Note the dramatic illustration of the "ripping robe," as the "robe of Samuel" has been seen before in chapter 2, and will be seen again in chapter 28. Why does Samuel refuse to accompany Saul, but then acquiesce? It is interesting that the "worship" itself is not recorded, but rather attention turns to the death of Agag.

9. Even though King Agag is put to death, this ancient rivalry between Israel and the Amalekites is not over. In fact, it will be replayed many years later during the period of the Exile, in the courts of Persia. The book of Esther describes the schemes of Haman (a descendant of "Agag"), as he seeks to destroy Mordecai (a descendent of "Kish") and his people. Do you notice any similarities between Agag and Haman?

10. As intimated above, the final sentence of chapter 15 provides a slight conflict of interpretation between the LORD and Samuel. Samuel tells Saul that God does not "regret/repent," but now the narrator informs the reader that "the LORD repented that he had caused Saul to become king over Israel." Does this serve to "destabilize" the prophet? Or is this an issue of minor consequence? Is God's "regret" over Saul's personal tragedy, or the way that Samuel treats Saul? Or is the nation's choice of kingship the reason for the divine sorrow? Is it possible that the rejection of Saul is somehow representative of Israel's rejection of divine kingship?

CHAPTER 16

NEW KID ON THE BLOCK

And the LORD said to Samuel, "How long will you be mourning over Saul? I've rejected him from being king over Israel. Fill your horn with oil and go. I'm sending you to Jesse of Bethlehem, for I've seen among his sons a king for me." Samuel said, "How can I go! Saul will hear, and kill me." The LORD said, "Take a heifer in your hand, and say, 'I've come for a sacrifice to the LORD.' Now, you'll invite Jesse to the sacrifice, and I will let you know what you should do, and you'll anoint for me that one whom I tell you."

And Samuel did as the LORD had spoken. He arrived at Bethlehem, and the elders of the city trembled as they met him. They said, "Have you come in peace?" Samuel said, "Yes, I've come to make a sacrifice to the LORD. Purify yourselves and come with me to the sacrifice." And he purified Jesse and his sons, then invited them to the sacrifice.

When they arrived, he saw Eliab, and said, "No doubt, before the LORD stands his anointed!" And the LORD said to Samuel, "Don't gaze on his appearance or the height of his stature, for I've rejected him—but not as a human would see: for humans pay attention to the eyes, but the LORD pays attention to the heart."

And Jesse called Abinadab, and passed him before Samuel. He said, "Moreover, this one the LORD hasn't chosen." So Jesse passed Shammah before him, and he said, "Moreover, this one the LORD

113

hasn't chosen." And Jesse passed seven of his sons before Samuel, and Samuel said to Jesse, "The LORD hasn't chosen any of these." Then Samuel said to Jesse, "Are these all the lads?" He said, "The smallest is left, but look, he's shepherding the flock!" Samuel said to Jesse, "Send and fetch him, for we won't turn around until he comes here."

So they sent, and brought him. He had a reddish-complexion, with beautiful eyes and good appearance. The LORD said, "Arise, anoint him, for this is he!" Then Samuel took the horn of oil and anointed him in the midst of his brothers, and the Spirit of the LORD rushed upon David from that day and onward. And Samuel arose and went to Ramah.

But the Spirit of the LORD turned aside from Saul, and an evil spirit from the LORD assailed him. The servants of Saul said to him, "Look, please, an evil spirit of God is assailing you. Let our lord speak to your servants before you, that they might seek a man who is a skillful harp player. So, when the evil spirit of God comes on you, he can play by hand, and you'll be better." And Saul said to his servants, "See if you can find for me, please, a man who is a good player, and bring him to me." One of the servant lads spoke up, and said, "Look, I've seen a son of Jesse from Bethlehem. He's a skillful player, a mighty warrior, a man of battle, a discerning speaker, and good-looking. And the LORD is with him."

Then Saul sent messengers to Jesse, and he said, "Send your son David to me, who is with the flock." So Jesse took a donkey—with food, a skin of wine, and a young goat—and sent it to Saul along with David. And David came to Saul, and stood before him, and he loved him greatly, and he became his weapons-carrier. Saul sent to Jesse, saying, "Please let David stand before me, for he's found favor in my eyes." As it happened, whenever the spirit of God was upon Saul, David took the harp and played with his hand. Saul was relieved, and felt better, and the evil spirit turned aside from him.

POINTS FOR REFLECTION:

1. As with chapters 13 and 15, a central issue of this chapter is "obedience" to the divine word. This time, though, it is the prophet Samuel who is directly involved. It is surely significant that Samuel condemns Saul for not *fully* obeying the "divine word" as he himself mediates it—yet God now gives Samuel a direct command, "Go to Bethlehem…" and Samuel refuses! Note carefully that in this chapter the prophet has his own struggles with implementing God's words, suggesting that it is more difficult than it appears. Does this cause the reader to have slightly more sympathy for Saul? As much as this chapter is about "calling a new king," it is also "a lesson in listening" for an older prophet. The chapter even begins with what seems to be a rebuke of the prophet, "How long…?" Does this imply that Samuel is not sufficiently focused on divine interests? Alter's comments (1999: page 95) should be carefully weighed:

> In the preceding episodes, the typical form of divine com-
> munication was Samuel's report of what God had said,
> although at Samuel's first sighting of Saul, a brief direct mes-
> sage from God is offered. As we have observed, these reports
> open up a certain margin of doubt as to whether the pur-
> ported divine injunctions are really God's or Samuel's. The
> present episode unfolds systematically through repeated dia-
> logue between God and Samuel, and so God's judgments are
> rendered with perfect, authoritative transparency. Evidently,
> the writer (or redactor) felt that the initial election of David
> had to be entirely unambiguous. As the story continues,
> God will no longer play this role of direct intervention.

2. Samuel complains, "Saul will hear, and kill me" yet nothing in the narrative thus far has indicated that Saul has lethal designs on Samuel. In fact, the opposite has been argued by some

115

commentators: Saul is terrified of Samuel. If this is so, then how should a reader understand Samuel's "disobedience" to God's direct command? What about the divine ruse that is designed for the prophet? Does the LORD call Samuel's bluff, or is something else going on?

3. Why do the elders of Bethlehem "tremble" as they go out to meet Samuel? Are they concerned that he has arrived in the city as a "judge" in his former capacity? Do they fear any (potential) political reprisals from such a visit? Or is this the normal reaction when a prophet comes to town? Does "Jesse" seem to be one of the town's elders? Incidentally, the Septuagint and one of the Qumran fragments (4QSam^b) reads "Have you come in peace, *O seer*?" This is interesting, as it plays on the verb "to see" which is a theme of this chapter: Samuel "the seer" has a "seeing" problem.

4. Upon seeing Eliab, Samuel does not comply with God's instructions. Samuel is directly commanded by the LORD, "anoint for me that one whom I tell you." Yet when he catches sight of Jesse's firstborn, he immediately says, "No doubt, before the LORD stands his anointed!" While some translations render this line as "Samuel's thought," it seems better to understand this as a public pronouncement. This is quite serious, as Samuel *could have* anointed the wrong candidate! How should the reader understand this "mistake" of the prophet? According to the strict criteria applied by the prophet to Saul in chapters 13 and 15, could the same be applied to Samuel and disqualify *him* from office? Are there different rules for prophet and king? Note carefully the divine rebuke: "Don't gaze on his appearance or the height of his stature, for I've rejected him—but not as a human would see: for humans pay attention to the eyes, but the LORD pays attention to the heart." How does this impact Samuel's characterization? Is this problem of

"seeing" simply something Samuel should be conscious of in the future, or has he been guilty of "acting according to the eyes" in the past?

5. How is David introduced, and why is this significant? It is conspicuous that God informs Samuel, "do not be misled by your eyes, as the outward appearance can be deceiving." Hence it is somewhat surprising that David has "beautiful eyes and good appearance"! How should the reader understand this tension? Is it a coincidence that the anointing of David occurs "in the exact middle of 1 Samuel?" (see Jobling 1998: 278).

6. In one of the most profound ironies, the Spirit rushes upon David, yet immediately turns aside from King Saul. This irony is intensified when (of all people!) *David himself* is invited to court and becomes a music therapist, and subsequently, the armor-bearer of Saul! The young man who has "secretly" been anointed king is now serving the incumbent monarch! Moreover, the description of David by "one of the servants" is quite remarkable. Is there any hyperbole in the servant's description? Where would such knowledge about David have been obtained? The servant does not mention David's name, yet when Saul sends a message to Jesse, he says, "Send your son *David* to me."

7. Incidentally, after anointing David, Samuel simply "goes to Ramah." Why is there an absence of instructions from the prophet, as there was with Saul in chapter 10? Nowhere does Samuel discuss any "signs," and he does not provide David with further instruction. Why is the prophet's conduct different with David than Saul? What does this suggest?

8. There is an interesting ambiguity in the line, "And David came

to Saul, and stood before him, *and he loved him greatly*, and he became his weapons-carrier." Who loves who? Compare the NRSV: "And David came to Saul, and entered his service. *Saul loved him greatly*, and he became his armor-bearer." The Hebrew text does not contain "Saul" as the subject, and although it is certainly possible to construe such a meaning, a slight ambiguity nonetheless remains.

9. The final picture in this chapter is David successfully ministering to Saul, and soothing the king during times of spiritual torment. David's musical talents will surface later in the narrative, along with his lyric gifts. Further, David's kindness to Saul provides something of a contrast to Samuel's rather harsh treatment, whether it is deserved or not. What does this image communicate to the reader? Is it a fitting conclusion to an astounding chapter? Is there any anticipation of the relationship between these two figures?

CHAPTER 17

PROFILES IN COURAGE

And the Philistines gathered their camp for battle, and assembled themselves at Socoh in Judah. They camped between Socoh and Azekah, in Ephes-dammim. Then Saul and the Israelites gathered, and camped in the valley of Elah. They arranged themselves in battle formation to meet the Philistines. So the Philistines were standing on one hill, and Israel on the other, with the valley between them.

And a Challenger marched out from the Philistine camp. His name was Goliath, from Gath. His height was six cubits and a span. A helmet of bronze was on his head, he was clothed with body-armor of scales. The weight of the body-armor was five thousand shekels of bronze. He had bronze leg-armor, and a bronze javelin was between his shoulders. The wood of his spear was like a weaver's beam, and its point weighed six hundred shekels of iron. His shield-carrier was walking before him. And he stood, and called aloud to the battle-ranks of Israel, and said to them, "Why have you marched out to align yourselves for battle? Aren't I the Philistine, and you the slaves of Saul? Pick a man for yourselves, and let him come down to me! If he's able to fight with me and strikes me down, then we'll become your slaves. But if I overcome him and strike him, then you'll become our slaves and you'll serve us!" And the Philistine said, "I've taunted the ranks of Israel today—give me somebody so we can fight together!" Saul and all Israel heard these words of the Philistines, and they were shattered, and greatly afraid.

Now David was the son of the Ephrathite, from Bethlethem of Judah, and his name was Jesse. He had eight sons, and during Saul's time the man was old and well-advanced in years. The three oldest sons of Jesse went to follow Saul in battle. The names of the three sons who went to battle were: Eliab, the firstborn, the second, Abinadab, and the third, Shammah. But David was the smallest, and the three older ones followed after Saul. And David would go back and forth from Saul, to shepherd his father's flock in Bethlehem. (Now the Philistine would draw near, morning and evening, for forty days, and take his stand.) And Jesse said to his son David, "Take your brothers this ephah of grain, along with these ten loaves of bread, and run to the camp, to your brothers. Also, bring these ten cheese cuts to the Commander of a the Unit. As for your brothers, inspect them to see if they're well, and get a guarantee from them. For Saul, and they, and all the Israelites were in the valley of Elah battling with the Philistines." So David got up early in the morning, left the flock with a keeper, packed up and went out just as Jesse commanded him. And he came to the trenches just when the army was marching out in battle formation, shouting the battle-cry.

Israel arranged themselves in battle formation to meet their opposing ranks. And David left the provisions under the care of the supplies-keeper, and ran to the battle lines. He arrived and asked his brothers if they were well. Now as he was speaking with them, look, the Challenger was coming up—named Goliath the Philistine, from Gath—from the battle ranks of the Philistines, and he spoke the same words as before. And David heard.

Now, when every Israelite saw the man, they fled from his presence, and they were terrified. Every Israelite was saying, "Do you see this man who is coming up? Indeed, to taunt Israel he's coming up! But the man who strikes him will be made wealthy by the king with lavish wealth. He'll give him his daughter in marriage, and his father's house will be free in Israel!" So David spoke to the men standing near him, saying, "What will be done for the man who strikes this Philistine and turns away this mockery from Israel? For who is this uncircumcised Philistine that he should mock the battle-ranks of the living God!" The troops spoke to him in the same way, saying, "Thus it will be done for the man who strikes him . . ." And his older brother Eliab heard him speaking with the men, and his anger burned against David, and he said, "Why is this you've come down? With whom have you left that little flock in the wilderness? *I'm* someone who knows your insolence and the evil in your heart. Indeed, you've come down in order to see the battle!" And David said, "What have I done now? Isn't it a word?" And he turned around from beside him toward someone else and spoke along a similar line, and the troops responded just as they had at first. But the words that David spoke were heard and reported to Saul, who fetched him.

And David said to Saul, "Don't let anyone lose heart—your servant will walk out and fight with this Philistine!" Saul said to David, "You aren't able to walk out and fight with this Philistine— for you're just a lad, but he's been a man of war *since* he was a lad!" David said to Saul, "Your servant has been a shepherd for his father's flock. Whenever a lion or bear would come and snatch up a sheep from the herd, I'd march out after him, strike him, and rescue it from its mouth. It would rise up against me, and I'd seize its beard, strike it and kill it. Your servant has struck both lion and bear—this uncircumcised Philistine will be like one of them, for he has taunted the battle-ranks of the living God!" And David said, "The LORD, who rescued me from the power of the lion and bear, he will rescue me from the power of this Philistine!" Saul said to David, "Go! And may the LORD be with you." And Saul clothed David in his apparel: he placed a bronze helmet on his head, and then suited him with body-armor. David strapped his sword over the apparel. He attempted to walk around, but could not even test it out. David said to Saul, "I'm unable to walk around in these—I can barely test it!" So David turned the garments aside. And he took his staff in his hand, and chose for himself five smooth stones from the wadi. He put them in the pocket of his shepherd's bag, and his slingshot was in his hand.

He drew near toward the Philistine. Then the Philistine approached, coming closer to David, with his shield-bearer before him. The Philistine looked and saw David, and despised him, for he was a lad with a reddish-complexion and good-looking. The Philistine said to David, "So, I'm a dog, and you're coming to me with sticks?" The Philistine cursed David by his gods. The Philistine said to David, "Come to me, and I'll give your flesh to the birds of the air and the beasts of the field!" David said to the Philistine, "You're coming against me with sword, spear, and javelin—but I'm coming against you in the name of the LORD of Hosts, the God of the battle-ranks of Israel who you've taunted! Today the LORD *will* hand you over to me, and I'll strike you and remove your head from upon you! On this day I'll give the corpse of the Philistine camp to the birds of the air and the creatures of the field, and all the earth will know that there is a God in Israel! This entire assembly will know that its not by sword or spear that the LORD saves—because the battle is the LORD's, and he's giving all of you into my hand!"

As the Philistine loomed tall and walked and drew near to meet David, David hurried and ran to the battle lines to meet the Philistine. David reached into his bag, took a stone out of it, slung it, and struck the Philistine in the head. The stone sunk into his forehead, and he fell on his face to the ground. Thus David triumphed over the Philistine with a slingshot and a stone. He struck the Philistine and killed him, and there was no sword in his hand. Then David ran and stood over the Philistine. He took his sword, drew it from its sheath, killed him, and cut off his head.

The Philistines saw that their warrior was dead, and they fled. And the men of Israel and Judah arose and gave a war-shout, and they pursued the Philistines until you approach the valley near the gates of Ekron. Philistine casualties were strewn along the road from Shaaraim as far as Gath and Ekron. Then Israelites returned from hotly pursuing the Philistines, and they looted their camp. And David took the head of Goliath, and brought it to Jerusalem, and placed the weapons in his own tent.

Now as Saul was watching David marching forth to meet the Philistine, he said to Abner, captain of the military, "Whose son is this lad, Abner?" Abner said, "On your life, O King, I don't know." The king said, "*You* ask whose son this stripling is." And, when David was returning from striking the Philistine, Abner took him and brought him before Saul, with the Philistine's head in his hand. Saul said to him, "Whose son are you, young man?" David said, "The son of your servant Jesse, from Bethlehem."

POINTS FOR REFLECTION:

1. This is a famous and familiar story, and even in a contemporary culture as illiterate as our own, "David and Goliath" continues to define the paradigm of the underdog. Despite its familiarity, I would suggest that this epic encounter has even deeper layers than most readers are aware of. Take, for instance, the description of Goliath and his armor—Alter refers to it as "Homeric," that is, the description is more reminiscent of the Iliad than classical Hebrew narrative. This could be exactly the note the author wants to sound, suggesting that this conflict is also about "worldviews at war." Consider this précis of a recent paper by Azzan Yadin, entitled "'Odysseus' Scar' Inscribed in I Samuel 17" (SBL 2001):

One of the best-known literary discussions of biblical narrative is Eric Auerbach's essay "Odysseus' Scar" in *Mimesis: The Representation of Reality in Western Literature*. In this influential work Auerbach distinguishes between a Homeric mode of representation in which the object or theme under discussion always receives the full attention of the narrator, on the one hand, and a biblical sensibility that is "fraught with background," that is, relegates to the background many key elements of the narrative. My presentation will argue that this distinction is, on some level, known and thematized by the biblical text itself. My focus is on the combat scene between David and Goliath in I Samuel 17, particularly the description of the Philistine champion, which includes a detailed analysis of Goliath's size, helmet, scale breast-plate, bronze breast-plate (and its weight), javelin, spear (and its weight), and even the shaft of the spear is discussed. Doubtless with Auerbach's distinction in mind, Robert Alter has noted (in *The David Story*) the "Homeric" nature of this passage. What are we to make of this very uncharacteristic narrative section? Using R. de Vaux's study on "Les combats singuliers dans l'Ancien Testament" as a guide, I will show that the "Homeric" style of the passage is not typical of battle scenes, suggesting the explanation for this narrative construction lies elsewhere. Where it lies, I would argue, is in recognizing that the Philistines were a Mycenaean-Greek nation that maintained its commercial and cultural ties with the "homeland" for many centuries. Clearly, it is not the historical Philistines as such that concern us here but their cultural representation in the eyes of the Deuteronomistic historian dating to perhaps the 7th century BCE (following Weinfeld) or later, as other scholars argue. In any case, there are explicit references to Homer's work in the 7th century

BCE, and Homer's floruit is traditionally dated to the 9th or 8th centuries. Thus, even the earlier datings of the Deutronomistic History allow for Israelite association of the Greek-Philistine with a Homeric (or Homer-like) literary tradition. Once this historical possibility has been laid out, the use of "Homeric" (again, it is Robert Alter's adjective) language to describe the Philistine (Greek-Mycenaean) hero can be understood in a new light. Namely, the Israelite author's description of Goliath as a mighty hero in good Homeric style subverts the (culturally dominant?) literary paradigms of Greek epic, ironically aggrandizing Goliath even as he is about to be slain by a sling-wielding shepherd. The encounter with the Philistines is, in this manner, framed not only as a political clash, but also as a struggle between two poetics, along much the same lines as Auerbach argued in "Odysseus' Scar." The literary aspect of this argument is two-fold. First, I am arguing that the Goliath narrative is best understood with Homer (or a generic "Homeric" style) as its intertextual other, following Bakhtin and Riffaterre on the last point. Second, the ironic modeling of the Philistine hero according to Homeric conventions suggests that Israel's struggle against the Philistines was seen as both political and cultural, and that the latter struggle is thematized in the most famous Israelite victory. Thus David's victory becomes the victory of the biblical poetic over that of the rival tradition.

Although this is a highly complex argument, what is your impression of the overall tenor of Yadin's proposal? In the Septuagint reading of Goliath's taunt "Aren't I a Philistine...?" a literal translation might be "Am I not a *foreigner*...?" David Jackson points out that the Septuagint also renders "Philistine" as *helleinas*, or "Hellenist" (SBL 2002). So, it may not be far-fetched to suggest that there are traces of a larger polemic against Greek culture in the "David vs. Goliath" epic battle. As you reflect on these matters, what else might be at stake in this contest?

2. Goliath is usually understood as a "champion," which is how a number of translations render the unique phrase "man-of-the-space-between" (the idea that the "last one standing" in the "space between" two armies is, logically enough, a champion—because he is still alive). I have rendered this phrase as a more technical term, "Challenger" (or "duelist/infantryman") based on the Qumran material, and because hand-to-hand combat seems to be Goliath's forte. "Gladiator" might be a stretch, although perhaps closer to the mark than one may expect.

3. Some scholars are puzzled by what they see as a "redundant, second introduction" to David. However, the focus on this second introduction is on Jesse. Jesse is pictured as highly concerned about the "well-being" of his three eldest sons (who at that very moment are paralyzed by the Philistine who "takes his stand"), and rather more casual with respect to David, who in the previous episode has been "anointed in the midst of his brothers." Why does the narrator pause to focus on Jesse at this key moment? Why is he so anxious that David "secure their pledge"? Does he seem less concerned about David?

4. The reader has actually waited a long time for the first words of David to be recorded in the narrative. He has now been on the scene for quite some time, yet the narrator has afforded him no direct speech. Now, on the battlefield, we hear his words for the first time. The speech itself is memorable and provocative, and serves as a remarkable foreshadowing of the David to come. It is as

126

though two different sides of David are being revealed here. First, he begins his speech by asking someone to reiterate what he has just heard, that is, the rewards offered for accepting this challenge: "What will be done for the man who strikes this Philistine and turns away this mockery from Israel?" As the youngest of eight brothers, his chances of material advancement through inheritance is limited. Thus David reveals himself as one who "opens the door when opportunity knocks"—and this knack for good "political" decisions will follow David throughout his early career. Second, David's stirring words—"For who is this uncircumcised Philistine that he should mock the battle-ranks of the living God!"—illustrates his soaring theological imagination. While the soldiers of Israel are paralyzed with fear, David has the requisite courage to remove the disgrace of the Philistine's insult. Where else do these two qualities (the political and the theological) of David's personality emerge as his career continues?

5. How should the words of Eliab, David's older brother be heard? On the one hand, his criticism can be heard as the ranting of a jealous older brother, and the kind of sibling rivalry that is popular in biblical narrative. On the other hand, he may be using hyperbole to sound a warning to David on this very public occasion. Notably, the word-clusters surrounding Eliab's speech resound at later points in the narrative, especially in 2 Samuel 11, the episode of David and Bathsheba, the murder of Uriah, and the parable of Nathan the prophet. The response of Eliab, then, is rather more complicated than many readers have appreciated. Does he provide any insight on David's *future* conduct? What is the purpose of Eliab's speech in this context?

6. Commentators have discussed the symbolism of Saul dressing David in his armor, which evokes earlier images of the Philistine's

weaponry. Evaluate these comments of Robert Alter (1992: 98-99):

> Goliath ...is introduced with a kind of Homeric recitation of battle equipment—bronze helmet, mail armor, bronze greaves and javelin, iron-tipped spear, and shield, with fabulous weights stipulated for most of the items on the list. We do not have to read much further to see why all this is here. When the young David volunteers to fight Goliath, Saul fits him out with his own armor and helmet and sword. The shepherd boy, however, stumbles under the unaccustomed weight of all these accouterments, puts them aside, and goes out to battle with his sling and five carefully chosen smooth stones. Just before he brings the Philistine giant crashing to the ground, he proclaims in his fighter's taunt to Goliath, "And all this assembly will know that neither by sword nor spear does the Lord grant victory, for the battle is the Lord's" (1 Sam. 17:47). ...The catalog of Goliath's armor begins to look like an allegorical satire on displaced faith in the realm of quantified material implements.

7. Incidentally, Gary Rendsburg (1999) comments on an unusual Hebrew verb form used for Saul dressing David in his armor. This highlights something odd about Saul's procedure for outfitting David: Saul does not place the helmet on David as the last item of armor. Rendsburg suggests that Saul is overwhelmed by David's offer to confront the Challenger, to the extent that he can barely even outfit his young soldier! This underscores, however subtly, the grim reality that if Israel loses this battle, they will be slaves to the Philistines. Consider Rendsburg's comments:

> Given the three items mentioned in this verse, the expected order of dressing would be "body-suit," "breastplate," and

128

finally "helmet." In the entire history of human armor, the last item to be donned is always the helmet. The most explicit evidence comes from the numerous textual references to the donning of armor in ancient and medieval literature (Iliad; La Chanson de Roland; and many other works), all of which refer consistently to the helmet as the last item to be affixed. One of the overall goals of the author of 1 Samuel, as many scholars have noted, is to show the inadequacy of Saul. The present passage should be understood as part of the portrayal. Saul's bewilderment at the presence of the shepherd boy David on the battlefield and his volunteering to fight Goliath has caused the king to become so flustered that he is unable even to dress another man properly. The language of 1 Sam 17:38 parallels the scene, both through the order of the objects mentioned and by use of the [verb] form "he placed" (clearly, the verb is not a perfect or a pluperfect here). I propose an English rendering of 1 Sam 17:38 such as "Saul clothed David in his body-suit, then he even placed a bronze helmet on his head, and he clothed him with a breastplate," with the highlighting ... verb indicated by the expression "then he even placed"; or more radically, "Saul clothed David in his body-suit, then placed he a bronze helmet on his head, and he clothed him with a breastplate," with the inverted word order "then placed he" replicating the most unusual presence of [this unexpected Hebrew verb form].

8. While Goliath may emerge as the ultimate "trash-talker," it appears that he meets his rhetorical match in the young Israelite who comes armed with "sticks" and a confidence in the God of Israel (and his own resourcefulness) that Goliath seriously underestimates. How do the words of David reflect his theological

129

imagination, and faith in the capacity of God to save Israel on this day? By the way, does the reader have any clues as to why David chose *five* stones? Did he lack confidence in his swinging ability? Or is the head of Goliath a rather big target that may require more than one rock to penetrate?

9. Speaking of Goliath's cranial capacity, an interesting detail that is often overlooked is the line, "And David took the head of Goliath, and brought it to Jerusalem." This is curious, because at this point in the story, Jerusalem is a Canaanite enclave in the midst of Israel. Otherwise known as "Jebus," this city was well-fortified, and the Israelites had not yet conquered it. This conceivably provides some insight on David's calculations for the future: even now, at this early point in his career, he has designs on this city as *his* capital. It would of course be a sensible choice, as it would be a "neutral" venue with an absence of political baggage and competing loyalties. Do you see David's action here as a shrewd calculation? How would the "Jebusites" feel when David marched into their city with the head of Goliath?

10. The final moments of this chapter provide something of a flashback to Saul's reactions as David is marching forth. Commentators are often troubled by this scene, where they believe that "Saul does not seem to know his own armor-bearer" of chapter 16. Since David and Saul have just been speaking in chapter 17, it is inconceivable that Saul is "suffering from amnesia" (as, in fact, has been suggested). At first glance, the questions are odd. A closer look, however, reveals that Saul is perhaps warning Abner to "keep an eye on this young upstart," since both Saul and Abner can potentially be threatened or undermined if the lad is successful. Do you think Saul has in mind the words of Samuel in chapter 15: "The LORD has ripped the kingdom of Israel from you today! He has

given it to your neighbor, one better than you." Does Saul suspect that David is "this neighbor"? Is this passage ironic in light of Saul later referring to David as "my son"?

CHAPTER 18

THE SPEAR OF FORESHADOWING

When David finished speaking to Saul, Jonathan's soul was bound with David, and Jonathan loved him like his own soul. Saul took him on that day, and did not allow him to return to his father's house. Jonathan and David cut a covenant, for he loved him as his own soul. Jonathan removed the robe that was upon him, and gave it to David, along with his armor, his sword, his bow, and his belt. And David marched out and was successful wherever Saul sent him. So Saul appointed him over the men of battle, which was good in the eyes of the troops, and even in the eyes of Saul's staff.

Now as they were coming in—when David was returning from striking the Philistine—the women marched out from the cities of Israel with singing and dancing, to meet King Saul with tambourines, joyful tunes, and triangles. The laughing women responded, and said, "Saul has struck his thousands, David his ten thousands!" This greatly burned Saul, and the thing was evil in his eyes. He said, "They've given 'ten thousands' to David, but to me they've given 'thousands.' Anything more would be the kingdom!" And Saul kept an eye on David from that point on.

The next day, an evil spirit from God rushed upon Saul, and he prophesied in the midst of his house. Now David was making music with his hand on that day, but the spear was in Saul's hand. And Saul hurled the spear, and said, "I'll strike right through David, and through the wall!" But David circled around him twice.

And Saul was afraid of David, for the LORD was with him, but from Saul he had turned aside. So Saul turned him aside from being near him, and appointed him as captain of a thousand. And he marched out and returned with the troops. On every journey, David was a success, and the LORD was with him. Saul saw that he was highly successful, and he dreaded him. But all Israel and Judah loved David, because he marched out and returned before them.

And Saul said to David, "Look! My older daughter Merab I'll give you for a wife—only be a valiant warrior for me, and fight the LORD's battles." But Saul was thinking, "Let my hand not be against him; rather, let the Philistines' hand be against him." David said to Saul, "Who am I? What's my life, or my father's family in Israel, that I should become a son-in-law to the king?" And when the time came to give Saul's daughter Merab to David, she was given as a wife to Adriel the Meholathite.

Now Michal, the daughter of Saul, loved David. This was reported to Saul, and the matter was upright in his eyes. And Saul said, "I'll give her to him, and she'll be a snare to him, and the Philistines' hand will be on him!" And Saul said to David for a second time, "Today you'll be my son-in-law." Saul commanded his staff, "Speak to David in secrecy, saying, 'Look! The king delights in you! All his servants love you! So now, be the king's son-in-law!'" And Saul's staff spoke these words in David's ears. David said, "Is it a trivial matter in your eyes to become the king's son-in-law? I'm a poor fellow, and lightly esteemed." Saul's staff reported to him, saying, "According to these words, David spoke." Saul said, "Thus say to David, 'The king desires no bride-price, only 100 Philistine foreskins to exact revenge on the king's enemies.'" (But Saul was calculating to cause David's fall by the hand of the Philistines.) His staff reported these words to David, and it was upright in David's eyes to become the king's son-in-law.

Now the time had not elapsed, so David arose, and went with his men and struck 200 Philistine males. David then brought the foreskins, and counted them out for the king in order to become the king's son-in-law. So Saul gave him his daughter Michal as a wife. Saul was afraid, and he knew that the LORD was with David, and that Saul's daughter Michal loved David. Saul grew even more afraid of David, and Saul was David's enemy all the time.

The Philistine captains marched forth, and every time they marched forth David was more successful than any of Saul's staff, and his name was highly valued.

POINTS FOR REFLECTION:

1. Barbara Green (2000: 81) suggests that *it is from Saul's point of view* that Jonathan "is bound" with David—and this same root occurs later, in Saul's direct speech, as "conspire." This puts Saul's later charge against his staff (chapter 22) in a rather different perspective. Green also notes the similar actions of Saul and Jonathan: both clothe David with weaponry (Fokkelman mentions that both son and father give four items to David), but with different results:

> Saul, who presumably remembers—or of whom we remember—his own clothing of David with royal gear, watches his son perform the same gesture unrebuffed. The actions of father and son are narratorially intertwined and placed here in anticipatory summary of some scenes that will be detailed as the story unfolds. (The narrator runs the tape forward in preview, so to speak.)

2. In chapter 16, music (from David) provides therapy for a

beleaguered King Saul. Here in chapter 18, music (about David) makes Saul angry. How does Saul construe the song? Is his "interpretation" correct? Are the singers treating David more importantly than Saul? The conventions of Hebrew poetry, one could argue, simply require the second poetic term to be significantly higher than the first term ("thousands . . . ten thousand"). Is it significant that while others are celebrating, Saul is seething with internal anger? How will this pattern unfold in the story? Further, why do all the people "love" David?

3. The (first) assassination attempt results in Saul placing David as the "captain of a thousand," the same number that "Saul has struck" according to the words of the women's song. What are some reasons why Saul would seek to kill David by hurling a spear at him? Comment on the theological implications of this line: "The next day, an evil spirit from God rushed upon Saul, and he prophesied in the midst of his house."

4. The (first) offer of marriage, one may have expected, should have come as a result of David's victory over the Philistine; now, Saul offers the hand of his older daughter, with the hope that the "Philistines" will eliminate David. Evaluate David's response, "Who am I...?" Is he posturing here, and concealing ambition? Or is he sincerely hesitant to join the royal family and acting in humility? Or does he not want Saul for a father-in-law because of the "spear incident" earlier in this chapter?

5. The (second) offer of marriage to Michal follows a similar pattern, with Saul hoping that she will be a "snare" or "trap" for David. The Hebrew term can also mean "bait" or "lure," and clearly the implication of Saul's thinking is that David will "fall" by the Philistines. Ironically, in the next chapter Michal will actually be

135

something of a "snare" for Saul himself!

6. Why is Saul so optimistic that the Philistines will kill David? So far, their champion's head has visited Jerusalem courtesy of David! Some commentators have detected "false modesty" in David's (second) refusal, especially since it is soon "upright in David's eyes to become the king's son-in-law." What exactly is going on in this transaction between Saul and David? Why is David not given his rewards *right after* killing Goliath?

7. David's fulfillment of the bride-price is surely comical as he counts out the rather appalling "trophies" right in front of Saul! Saul's reaction is not given, but the narrator stresses the king's growing "fear" of David. Evaluate this episode in light of the larger development of Saul and David's relationship. Why is the reader informed, twice, that Michal "loves" David? Why does this scare her father Saul?

CHAPTER 19

A Son-in-law is Hard to Find

And Saul spoke to his son Jonathan and all his staff, in order to put David to death. But Saul's son Jonathan greatly delighted in David. Jonathan reported to David, saying, "My father Saul is seeking to put you to death. So now, be careful in the morning—stay in a secret place, and hide yourself. I myself will go out and stand next to my father in the field where you are. I'll speak to him about you, and whatever I see I'll report to you." So Jonathan spoke well of David to his father Saul, and said to him, "Let the king not sin against his servant David, for he hasn't sinned against you— rather his deeds for you have been very good! He took his life in his hands and struck the Philistine, and the LORD accomplished a great salvation for all Israel—you saw, and you rejoiced! Why are you sinning against innocent blood by gratuitously putting David to death?" Saul listened to the voice of Jonathan, and Saul swore an oath, "As the LORD lives, he won't be put to death." And Jonathan called to David, and Jonathan reported to him all these words. Then Jonathan brought David to Saul, and he was in his presence just like previous times.

Again war broke out, and David marched forth and battled against the Philistines. He struck them with a heavy attack, and they fled from him. Then an evil spirit of the LORD was upon Saul. He was sitting in his house with his spear in his hand, and David was making music with his hand. Saul tried to strike the spear through

David and through the wall, but he eluded Saul, and the spear struck the wall. But David fled, and that night he was able to slip away.

Saul sent agents to David's house in order to keep watch and kill him in the morning. His wife Michal reported this to him, saying, "If you don't slip away tonight, then tomorrow you're a dead man." And Michal lowered David out through a window, and he went out and fled and slipped away. Then Michal took the Teraphim idol and set it on the bed, along with a quilt of goat's hair that she placed at its head, and covered it with a garment. Saul sent agents to apprehend David, and she said, "He's sick." So Saul sent the agents to view David, saying, "Bring him up to me on the bed to kill him." The agents came in, but look, the Teraphim idol was on the bed, with a quilt of goat's hair at its head! Then Saul said to Michal, "Why have you deceived me like this, and let my enemy go, and he has slipped away?" Michal said to Saul, "He said to me, 'Let me go! Why should I kill you?'"

But David fled, and made his escape. He came to Samuel at Ramah, and reported to him all that Saul had done to him. So he and Samuel went and stayed at Naioth. It was reported to Saul, saying, "Look, David is at Naioth in Ramah." And Saul sent agents to apprehend David. But when they saw the company of prophets prophesying with Samuel standing as a pillar over them, the Spirit of God was upon the agents of Saul, and they too prophesied. This was reported to Saul, so he sent other agents, but these also prophesied. Saul continued to send a third group of agents, but they also prophesied. So he himself went to Ramah. He came to the great well of Secu, and asked, and said, "Where are Samuel and David?" One said, "Look, in Naioth of Ramah." He went there—to Naioth of Ramah—and the Spirit of God also came upon him, and he prophesied as he walked along until he came to Naioth of Ramah. He also stripped off his garments and prophesied before

Samuel, and fell naked all that day and night. That is why they say, "Is *even* Saul among the prophets?"

POINTS FOR REFLECTION:

1. In this chapter Saul has *two* of his children covertly work for David over and against him. How does this serve to intensify the king's growing sense of alienation? Moreover, Saul's pursuit of David in this chapter sets in motion the game of "hide and seek" that is a major component of the narrative for the foreseeable future. Jonathan's actions on behalf of David remind us of an earlier question: why does everyone love David? Is it his "handsome appearance" or the fact that "the LORD is with him"? In chapter 16, Saul "loved" David—why is he now obsessed with destroying his highly successful military captain?

2. Evidently Jonathan underestimates his father, since there is a reversion to "spear-throwing" behavior. What about the fact that Saul "swore an oath" by the LORD? Note that this scene is crafted in a very similar manner to chapter 18, especially the detail of Saul with his "spear in his hand." This detail now becomes an instrument of foreshadowing whenever it occurs again in the narrative.

3. In chapter 18, the betrothal controversy with Merab and Michal—older and younger—activates an allusion to the Leah and Rachel episodes in the book of Genesis. The allusions to Genesis are more acute here in chapter 19. There is a network of correspondences between Genesis 31 (Jacob fleeing from Laban, and Rachel stealing the *Teraphim* idol) and here in 1 Samuel 19 (David fleeing from Saul, and Michal aiding his escape through a

Teraphim idol). Both of these episodes feature *angry father-in-laws* (Saul and Laban), *younger daughters* (Michal and Rachel), *fugitive husbands* (David and Jacob) and *deceptive idols* (Michal covers the idol in hair to fool Saul's agents, and Rachel hides her fathers *Teraphim* under her camel's saddle). See the comments of Robert Alter (*The David Story*, 120):

> The household gods are what Rachel stole and hid from her father when Jacob fled from him. Like Rachel, who pleads her [indisposition] and does not get up from the cushions under which the *teraphim* are hidden, Michal also invokes "illness" [1 Sam 19:14] to put off the searchers. Both stories feature a daughter loyal to her husband and rebelling against a hostile father. Michal puts goat's hair at the head of the bed because, being black or dark brown, it would look like a man's hair, but goats (and the color of their hair) are also prominent in the Jacob story. Laban, of course, never finds his *teraphim*, whereas Saul's emissaries, to their chagrin, find the *teraphim* instead of the man they are looking for.

What is the significance of the connection and clear parallel with Genesis here? How does it impact the various levels of plot, characterization, and theology? Does this allusion suggest to the reader that David will have "family problems" similar to Jacob? Incidentally, later in the narrative the reader discovers that Merab gives birth to numerous children (a possible allusion to Leah) while Michal does not (a possible allusion to the earlier career of Rachel). Compare the dialogue of Michal and Rachel with Saul and Laban. How does Michal emerge from this scene?

4. Why does David flee to Samuel? These two rarely come in contact, and this seems to be the first recorded occasion since the anointing of chapter 16. Is David keeping his distance from

Samuel? Do they get together again after this? Why is Samuel so active during Saul's (brief) reign, yet so passive with David?

5. In the final scene of this dramatic chapter, Saul is once more "asking" for directions just as in chapter 9. There is a powerful connection between his earlier "prophetic" activity and this present scene, most vividly in the reoccurrence of the question, "Is *even* Saul among the prophets?" However, there are also several poignant differences between the scene, as graphically Saul strips off his (royal) garments. Hamilton (2001: page 267) notices that Samuel predicts Saul's first encounter with the prophets (in chapter 10), but not this second one. Hamilton also summarizes other commentators:

> Brueggemann (1990: 45) observes that the "pitifully embarrassing scene is that of this once great man, still tall but no longer great … now rendered powerless in a posture of submissiveness." … Jobling (1978: 10) quotes the German scholar Stoebe: "The clothes which are here torn off are the clothes of a king, who now, not only in disgraceful nakedness, but stripped likewise of power, lies impotently on the ground."

Finally, the reader should keep in mind that this is not the last time that Samuel and Saul will meet, nor is it the final occasion where Saul will be lying down on the ground before Samuel. How does this episode reflect on Saul? Why is it that David does not join in the "prophesying" whereas Saul does (both here and in chapter 10)? What exactly does "prophesying" mean? How is it that Saul prophesies even though the LORD has turned aside from him?

CHAPTER 20

WHEN THE REIGN STARTS TO FALL

And David fled from Naioth of Ramah, and came before Jonathan, and said, "What have I done? What's my guilt? How have I sinned before your father that he's seeking my life?" He said, to him, "No way—you'll not be put to death! Look, my father doesn't do anything, great or small, without revealing it to me. Why would my father keep *this thing* secret from me? It can't be!" David then swore an oath, and said, "Your father surely knows that I've found favor in your eyes, so he thinks, 'Jonathan must not know about this matter, lest he get hurt.' But as the LORD lives, and as you live, there's only one step between me and death!" Jonathan said to David, "I'll do whatever you say."

David said to Jonathan, "Look, tomorrow is a new month, and I'm supposed to sit down with the king to eat. Now, release me and I'll conceal myself in the field until the third evening. If your father takes account of me, then say, 'David earnestly asked me if he could run to Bethlehem his city, for an annual sacrifice is happening there for all his family.' If he says, 'Great!' then all is well with your servant. But if his anger is kindled, then know for certain that he's bent on evil. But you have to act with loyalty to your servant, for you've brought your servant into a covenant of the LORD. So if there's any guilt in me, then put me to death yourself—why wait to bring me to your father?" Jonathan said, "Absolutely not! If I knew for sure that my father was bent on bringing evil on you, wouldn't

I report it to you?" David said to Jonathan, "Who will report to me if your father responds harshly?" Jonathan said to David, "Come on, let's go to the field." And the two of them went out to the field.

Jonathan said to David, "By the LORD God of Israel, indeed I'll sound out my father around this time tomorrow or the third day if he is positive toward David. But if not, I'll send to you and reveal it to your ear. So may the LORD do to Jonathan and even more if it pleases my father to harm you, and I don't reveal it to your ear and send you off that you may go in peace! And may the LORD be with you just as he was with my father. If I live, won't you act with the loyalty of the LORD toward me, or if I die? Don't ever cut off your loyalty toward my house, not even when the LORD cuts off all of David's enemies from the face of the earth. And so Jonathan has cut a deal with the house of David and may the LORD seek it from the hand of David's enemies."

And again Jonathan made David swear an oath out of his love for him, for he loved him as his own soul. Then Jonathan said to him, "Tomorrow is a new month, and you'll be missed since your seat will be empty. When you've waited three days, go a long way down and head to the place where you hid yourself on the day of that business, and stay near Ezel Rock. I'll shoot three arrows beside it, like I was shooting at a target. Right at that moment I'll send the lad, 'Go, find the arrows!' If I say to the lad, 'Look! the arrows are on *this* side of you. Take them!' then you can go, for all is well, and as the LORD lives, there's nothing. But if I say to the youngster, 'Look, the arrows are further away from you,' then go, for the LORD is sending you off. And as for the matter that you and I spoke of, the LORD is between you and I forever."

And David hid himself in the field. The new month arrived, and the king sat down to eat at the feast. The king was seated in his usual place near the wall. Jonathan arose, and Abner sat down beside Saul. David's place was empty. Now Saul did not say anything on that day, for he thought, "Something's happened to him, and he's unclean. Surely he's unclean." On the next day (the second day of the new month), David's place was empty. And Saul said to his son Jonathan, "Why hasn't the son of Jesse come to the feast either yesterday or today?" Jonathan answered Saul, "David earnestly asked me about Bethlehem. He said, 'Please let me go, for there's a family sacrifice in the city. My brother has commanded me. So now, if I've found favor in your eyes, let me slip away so I can see my brothers.' That's why he hasn't come to the king's table."

And Saul's wrath was kindled against Jonathan, and he said to him, "You son of a twisted and rebellious woman! Don't I know that you've chosen the son of Jesse to your shame and the shame of your mother's nakedness? Indeed, every day that the son of Jesse lives on the earth, neither you or your kingdom will be established. So now, send and fetch him to me, for he's a son of death!" Jonathan answered his father Saul, and said to him, "Why should he be put to death? What has he done?" And Saul hurled his spear at him, to strike him. Then Jonathan knew that his father was bent on putting David to death. And Jonathan arose from the table, hot with rage. He did not eat on the second day of the new month, for he was grieved about David, for his father had humiliated him.

In the morning Jonathan went out to the field at the time appointed with David, and a small lad was with him. He said to the lad, "Run! Please find the arrows that I've shot." The boy ran, and he shot the arrow beyond him. As the boy came to the spot where Jonathan shot the arrow, Jonathan called after him and said, "Isn't the arrow further away from you?" Jonathan called after the lad, "Hurry! Make haste! Don't stand there!" And the lad gathered up the arrows and came to his master. (Now the lad did not know anything, only Jonathan and David were aware of the matter.) And Jonathan gave his weapons to the lad, and said to him, "Go, bring them to the city."

As the lad went, David arose from Ezel of the South. He fell on his face to the ground, and bowed down three times. Each kissed the other, and each wept for his friend, until David was greater. Jonathan said to David, "Go in peace, because both of us have sworn an oath in the name of the LORD, saying, 'May the LORD be between me and you, and between my descendants and yours forever.'"

POINTS FOR REFLECTION:

1. Jonathan's trust in Saul is matched by David's skepticism—of course, the latter has had a spear thrown at his head on multiple occasions, which would no doubt engender such skepticism. The initial exchange between David and Jonathan features a number of questions and rebuttals. Is David trying to convince Jonathan of Saul's malevolence toward him? What would be the purpose of David's "plan" about going to Bethlehem for a family sacrifice? Some commentators have sensed that David may be slightly manipulating Jonathan here. Do you agree, or is this assessment off the mark? Robert Alter notes that these are David's first reported words to Jonathan, which is rather surprising. What is the result of such narrative delay?

2. If the first "scene" in chapter 20 has more discourse from David, the second scene (outside, in the field) is predominantly Jonathan. At least two things emerge from Jonathan's lengthy speech and "arrow" plan. First, his connection with David is becoming increasingly hazardous. The elaborate precautions seem to indicate that he must sense that David is right about Saul. Second, it is ironic that his reference to "David's enemies" must include his own father! Do you sense that Jonathan might be aware of this?

3. As the scene switches to the "new moon" feast Saul is positioned "by the wall," a wall which may be punctured with spear-marks. This small detail of "the wall" thus provides a flashback to chapters 18 and 19 (when Saul hurls his spear at David, attempting to frame his portrait, as it were) and also foreshadows another of Saul's violent outbursts (this time with Jonathan himself the target). Note that Saul first is depicted through an *internal monologue*, as he theorizes that David is "not clean." Why is Saul concerned about David's absence? Does he fear that David is "up to something"?

4. After hearing Jonathan's explanation for David's absence, Saul's reaction is vehement. His insult of Jonathan is extreme by any standard—how does this reflect on Saul as a father? Fokkelman notes a connection between Jonathan's casual use of the verb "slip away" and its earlier uses in chapter 19. It is notable that both brother and sister are involved with this same term with respect to David. In light of the "bed-trick" scene featuring Michal in chapter 19, Jonathan's use of the verb must be particularly grating to Saul. What is Saul's point to Jonathan about "your kingdom" in light of Samuel's words that he will not sire a dynasty? Consider Barbara Green's comments (2000: 126):

> Saul has stated his priority, which is to leave his son Jonathan to rule; it is a subset of his main drive, which is to remain king. Saul sets the problem in terms of Jonathan's shaming his mother and names David as the obstacle. He avoids saying that Jonathan's actions shame him and that he has been told that the obstacle to Jonathan's rule is God's preference. Even at his most forthright moment, he leaves a great deal submerged. Blaming at very least Jonathan and David, Saul refuses to acknowledge his own role for what it

is. David's life on earth is a threat to Saul's rule as well as Jonathan's, a situation Saul has been acting on for several scenes. That his own actions have obviated his goal Saul does not acknowledge.

5. Describe how this line contributes to Jonathan's characterization in the narrative: "And Jonathan arose from the table, hot with rage. He did not eat on the second day of the new month, for he was grieved about David, for his father had humiliated him." Who is the "him" in the last part of the line, "for his father had humiliated *him*"? Is it Jonathan, or David? What is the effect either way?

6. As the chapter closes with a final scene of the two friends, the reader notices that "oath-language" is again at the forefront of Jonathan's discourse. Why is Jonathan interested in securing an oath from David? What reason does he have to fear for the safety of his descendants? Evaluate this comment of Peter Miscall (1986: page 130-31):

> Jonathan and David are close friends and are bound by a covenant that extends to descendants (vv. 12-17, 42). Jonathan demands an oath from David sealing the covenant because of his sincere love for his friend or because of his fear of David's violence. Jonathan has sufficient experience to know the violence and irrationality that his father is capable of and may fear the same of David if David prevails in the conflict with Saul.

CHAPTER 21

CONSPIRACY THEORIES

And he arose and went, and Jonathan entered the city. David came to Nob, to Ahimelech the priest. Ahimelech trembled to meet David, and said to him, "Why are you alone, and no one is with you?" David said to Ahimelech the priest, "The king has charged me with something, and he said to me, 'No one is to know anything about where I'm sending you or what I've charged you.' As for the young lads, I've let them know about a certain unnamed place. So now, what have you got? Give me five loaves of bread, or whatever can be found."

The priest answered David, and said, "I haven't got any ordinary bread, there is only holy bread *if* the young lads have kept themselves from women." David answered the priest, and said to him, "Indeed women have been kept from us as with previous times I've marched out. The vessels of the young lads are holy even if the journey is common—so how much more today will the vessels be holy!" And the priest gave him the holy object, for there was not any bread there expect for the bread of the presence, which is removed from before the LORD and replaced with hot bread on the day it is taken.

Now one of Saul's staff was there on that day, detained before the LORD. His name was Doeg the Edomite, head of Saul's shepherds. And David said to Ahimelech, "Have you got in your possession a spear or sword? Indeed, my own sword and weapons I wasn't able to even take, for the king's word was urgent." The priest said, 'The sword of Goliath the Philistine, whom you struck down in the valley of Elah, look, its wrapped up in some clothes behind the ephod. If you want to take it, go ahead, for there's nothing else here except that one." David said, "There's none like it! Let me have it."

And David arose and on that day he fled from the presence of Saul, and came to Achish king of Gath. Achish's staff said to him, "Isn't this David, king of the land? Isn't he the one they sing to each other about in their dances, saying, 'Saul has struck his thousands, David his ten thousands'?" So David took these words to heart, and he was very afraid in the presence of Achish king of Gath. And he altered his behavior before their eyes, and while he was in their hand he acted like a lunatic. He began scratching the doors of the gate, and spittle ran down his beard. Achish said to his staff, "Look, do you see this man's madness? Why have you brought him to me? Am I lacking in madmen that you would bring this one to act the madman before me? Does this fellow *have to* enter my house?"

POINTS FOR REFLECTION:

1. Why does David travel to the priestly city of Nob, and specifically why does he go "to Ahimelech the priest" as he flees from Saul? Is Ahimelech an ally? Ahimelech's interrogation of David is fraught with suspicion. The sanctuary at Nob appears to be a dangerous place. Why is this? Details will emerge in due course, and the reader will learn *possible reasons* for the "trembling" of Ahimelech.

2. David's explanation about why he is alone certainly sounds dubious, as the reader is well aware. The rather vague and equivocal language gives David's words the pungent aroma of an excuse that

is fabricated on the spot. But why would he *need* to do this if Ahimelech is an ally? Perhaps it has something to do with the menacing presence of "Doeg the Edomite," who for undefined reasons is lurking in the sanctuary shadows.

3. In a study of this passage, Pamela Reis contends that there is a "collusion at Nob," that is, David and Ahimelech speak in covert language to mislead Doeg. Thus, when Ahimelech comes "trembling" to meet David, it is because one of Saul's high-ranking officials is present. David's speech illustrates that he takes Ahimelech's hint, and is intentionally vague. Evaluate the plausibility of Reis' thesis. Is it convincing?

4. There is a nice example of "delayed exposition" as Doeg is introduced a considerable time *after* the start of the scene. Thus, the reader is invited to "revise" the previous dialogue between David and the priest and factor in the presence of Doeg the Edomite. The reference to the weapon of Goliath further cements the idea that David and Ahimelech are allies. First, at the end of chapter 17 David is in possession of Goliath's weapons, so it seems reasonable that at some point he deposited them in Nob. Second, Ahimelech's words "The sword of Goliath the Philistine, *whom you struck down in the valley of Elah*" seem calculated to inject some fear into Doeg. Is Ahimelech trying to throw Doeg off the scent? Or is he suggesting that David eliminate this potential adversary as soon as possible? Does this moment serve to foreshadow Doeg's next visit to Nob (chapter 22) where he will be armed with the sword?

5. Do you agree that there is some humor in the fact that David flees to (of all places) the city of Gath, Goliath's hometown? Thus armed with the giant's sword, David strolls into the heart of Philistine territory. He is apparently so afraid of Saul that he has to

seek refuge in the place where Goliath himself was born and raised. Moreover, there seems to be some darker humor in this episode: while fleeing from Saul, David feigns madness in Gath; while seeking David's life, Saul experiences bouts of genuine madness.

6. Noticeably, those "lyrics" celebrating David and Saul's triumph in battle surface again. On this occasion there is quite an irony in that the lyrics are quoted *by the Philistines*, since it was *their* defeat that provided the reason for the song to be written in the first place! Just like this song arouses suspicion in Saul, so Achish's staff quote the lyrics to support their distrust of David (whom they view as "the king of the land"). The speech-patterns of Achish, and the tension between him and his staff, are issues to keep in the mind for future scenes in the narrative.

CHAPTER 22

THE FUGITIVE

And David went from there and slipped away to the Cave of Adullam. His brothers and his father's household heard of this, and they came down to him there. A group assembled around him—anyone who was in a difficult situation, or in debt, or bitter-in-spirit—and he became their captain. About 400 men were with him.

Then David went on from there to Mizpeh of Moab. He said to the king of Moab, "Please let my mother and father come out to you, until I know what God intends to do with me." So he left them with the king of Moab, and they stayed with him the whole time that David was in the stronghold.

Then Gad the prophet said to David, "Don't stay in the stronghold. Go, enter the land of Judah." So David went and entered the forest of Hereth. Saul heard that David was identified, and that men were with him. Now Saul was sitting in Gibeah, under the tamarisk-tree on the hill. His spear was in his hand, and members of his staff were standing around him. Saul said to his staff standing around him, "Listen to me, men of Benjamin! Will the son of Jesse give to every one of *you* fields and vineyards? Will every one of *you* be appointed as captains of thousands or hundreds? For you've all conspired against me! None of you have revealed to my ear that my son cut a deal with the son of Jesse, and none of you has pity on me and reveals to my ear that my son has incited my servant against me to lie in ambush as he does today!

Then Doeg the Edomite spoke up (he was standing among Saul's staff), and he said, "I saw the son of Jesse come to Nob, to Ahimelech son of Ahitub. He inquired of the LORD for him, gave him provisions, and gave him the sword of Goliath the Philistine." Then Saul sent a dispatch to call Ahimelech son of Ahitub the priest, and his father's entire house, the priests of Nob. All of them came to the king. Saul said, "Listen to me, son of Ahitub!" He said, "Here I am, my lord." Saul said to him, "Why have you conspired against me, you and the son of Jesse? You gave him food and a sword, and inquired of God for him to rise up against me, to lie in ambush this very day!" Ahimelech answered the king and said, "Who, among all your staff, is like David: reliable, the king's son-in-law, one who inclines to your counsel and is honored in your house? Today did I begin to inquire of God for him? Far be it from me! Don't let the king charge anything against his servant or my father's house, for your servant didn't know anything in all of this, great or small!"

The king said, "You *will* surely die Ahimelech, you and your father's entire house!" The king said to his escorts standing around him, "Turn around and kill the priests of the LORD, for their hand is with David. Moreover, they knew that he was fleeing, and didn't reveal it to my ear." But Saul's staff was unwilling to send their hands to fall upon the priests of the LORD. Then Saul said to Doeg, "You turn around and fall upon the priests." And Doeg the Edomite turned around, and fell upon the priests, and that day he put to death 85 men who carried the linen ephod. He also struck Nob, the city of priests, with the mouth of the sword: man and woman, children and nursing babies, cattle, donkeys and sheep, all with the mouth of the sword.

But a single son of Ahimelech son of Ahitub was able to slip away. His name was Abiathar, and he fled after David. Abiathar reported to David that Saul killed the priests of the LORD. David said to Abiathar, "I knew that Doeg the Edomite was there on that day, and that he'd be sure to tell Saul. I'm the one who has turned around against the life of your father's house! Stay here with me. Don't be afraid, for the one who seeks your life also is seeking my life. Indeed, you'll be under guard with me."

POINTS FOR REFLECTION:

1. Is it incidental that this chapter commences with those estranged from Saul or "bitter of spirit" gathering around David? What about the fact that he courts sponsorship (to some degree) from yet another foreign king? Clearly leaders such as Achish (in the future) and the king of Moab (in the present) are not acting out of charity. Why is it in their "enlightened self-interest" to assist David at this time?

2. What is Gad the prophet doing with David? Why is Samuel not with him? The presence of Gad contrasts somewhat with Saul's situation, most noticeably in that Gad immediately proffers "divine intelligence" to David. Comment on the discrepancy of Saul's *lack of divine response* and Gad's presumably unprompted sharing of the divine will with David.

3. The image of Saul sitting under the tree "spear in hand" is by now an ominous image. His staff, in probability, would prefer that the spear not be hurled in their direction. What is communicated through Saul's language here? What options does he set before his staff?

4. When Doeg the Edomite speaks up, it is evident that he was

well aware of David's visit to Nob in the previous chapter. His testimony before Saul is most intriguing. Note that Doeg "adds" one item: he tells Saul that the priest "inquired" (again, a wordplay on Saul's name, "ask") of the LORD for David. Since there is no record of an inquiry in chapter 21, the reader has to wonder if Doeg's account is false, and if he is trumping up the charges. What would be Doeg's motive for such an elaboration? Or is it possible that he is telling the truth? In light of Saul's failure with such "inquiries," this must be particularly galling.

5. When Ahimelech is summoned before Saul, the reader recalls that he is a member of the doomed house of Eli. Since chapter 2 the house of Eli has been under divine judgment. As he testifies before Saul, how does he emerge in your mind? Is he covering up for David (proving that indeed there was a "collusion at Nob")? Or has he been fooled by David's "excuses" in the previous chapter? Comment on his "defense" of David before the king. Also note a stunning contrast: Saul's staff are unwilling to lay a hand on the priests, yet Doeg "the Edomite" betrays no such scruple.

6. When Abiathar, the sole survivor, flees to David for refuge, again the prophetic words of chapter 2 come to mind: "...But one man I will not cut off for you from my altar, so that your eyes will fail and your soul grieve, and all the increase of your house will die as men... And it will be that any who are leftover in your house will come to bow down ... for a payment of silver or a loaf of bread, and say, 'Attach me, please, to one of the priestly offices, so as to eat a morsel of bread.'" David's comments reveal that he was well aware of Doeg's foreboding presence at Nob. Evaluate David's response to Abiathar. What is he saying? Miscall (1986: 137) comments as follows:

155

David accepts the blame, and the violence of the sword remains attached to him. His acceptance is a statement of fact, not necessarily an admission of guilt, since he says no more of it, nor does he bewail the catastrophe. Whatever David's opinion of his involvement in the slaughter of Abiathar's family, the episode ends with Abiathar bound to David for his protection.

CHAPTER 23

ORACLE SOFTWARE

Then they reported to David, saying, "Look, Philistines are battling against Keilah, and they're plundering the threshing-floors!" And David inquired of the LORD, saying, "Should I go up and strike these Philistines?" The LORD said to David, "Go up and strike the Philistines, and save Keilah." Then David's men said to him, "Look, here in Judah we're afraid, and now we're supposed to go to Keilah against the battle-ranks of the Philistines?" So David once again inquired of the LORD. The LORD answered him. and said, "Arise, go down to Keilah, for I'm giving the Philistines into your hand." So David and his men went to Keilah and battled against the Philistines. He drove their livestock away, and struck them heavily. Thus David saved the inhabitants of Keilah. (Now when Abiathar son of Ahimelech was fleeing to David, he came down with the ephod in his hand.)

It was reported to Saul that David had come to Keilah. Saul said, "God has alienated him into my hand! Indeed, he's closed himself in by entering a city with doors and bars." Then Saul summoned the troops for battle, to go down to Keilah and lay a siege for David and his men. David knew that Saul was devising evil against him, and he said to Abiathar the priest, "Bring the ephod here." David said, "O LORD God of Israel, your servant has definitely heard that Saul is seeking to come to Keilah, to destroy the city because of me. Will the leaders of Keilah hand me over to him? Will Saul come down just as your servant has heard? O LORD God of Israel, please report to your servant!" The LORD said, "He will come down." David said, "Will the leaders of Keilah hand me and my men into the hand of Saul?" The LORD said, "Yes." So David and his men, about 600, arose and marched out of Keilah, wandering around wherever they could. It was reported to Saul that David slipped out of Keilah, and he stopped marching forth.

And David dwelt in the wilderness, in the strongholds. He stayed in the mountain area of the wilderness of Ziph. Saul sought him constantly, but God did not give him into his hand. David saw that Saul was marching out to seek his life, and David was in the wilderness of Ziph at Horesh. Then Saul's son Jonathan arose and went to David at Horesh, and strengthened his hand in God. He said to him, "Don't be afraid, for my father's hand won't find you. But you'll indeed reign over Israel and I'll be your second-in-command. Even Saul my father knows this!" The two of them cut a covenant before the LORD. And David stayed at Horesh, while Jonathan went to his house.

Then the Ziphites went up to Saul at Gibeah, saying, "Isn't David hiding among us in the strongholds of Horesh, on Hachilah Hill south of Jeshimon? So now, if your soul should desire it, O king, then come on down, and we'll hand him over to the king's hand." Saul said, "May you be blessed by the LORD for having compassion on me! Please go and establish, make sure, and determine the place where his foothold is. Who has seen him there? For I've been told that he is exceptionally crafty. So determine and know every hiding place where he conceals himself. Return to me with confirmation, and I'll go with you. If he's in the land, then I'll dig him out among all the thousands of Judah!" Then the Ziphites arose and left Saul's presence.

Now David and his men were in the wilderness of Maon, in the Arabah south of Jeshimon. Saul and his men left for the search, but it was reported to David, and he went down to the cliffs and stayed in the wilderness of Maon. Saul heard, and pursued after David to the wilderness of Maon. Saul went on one side of the mountain, while David and his men were on the other side. David was hurrying to get away from Saul's presence, but Saul and his men were encircling David and his men to capture them. But then an agent came to Saul, saying, "Quick! Go! For the Philistines are raiding the land!" And Saul turned back from the pursuit of David, and went to meet the Philistines. That is why the place is named Rock of Divisions.

POINTS FOR REFLECTION:

1. This chapter begins with a disproportionate amount of "oracular" inquiry. Notably, this episode comes right after the massacre of Nob, where Saul is probably incensed by discussion of David receiving a divine oracle. This serves to underscore a growing subplot of "seeking divine knowledge" during David's fugitive era, and also highlights Saul's lack of divine response. Many commentators point out that an "oracle" answer is usually binary, "yes or no." Observe that in this chapter David receives some rather loquacious divine responses on a couple of occasions. There is a pointed contrast, then, between David and Saul during this narrative stretch, and the growing theme of David's impressive oracular success versus Saul's growing frustration and failure (that will culminate in chapter 28). Curiously, something similar happens in Judges 20 (Israel vs. Benjamin). Does Judges 20 foreshadow 1 Samuel 23, or is this just a coincidence?

2. David's men have grave misgivings about traveling to Keilah in order to battle the Philistines. It is convenient, therefore, that David

is able to procure an oracle for "political" reasons, and reassure his men *by means of the oracle* that it is safe to travel there. Again, David's success in this regard contrasts with Saul's lack of success.

3. There is another nice piece of "delayed exposition" as the narrator discloses that Abiathar had turned up in David's camp with a piece of "oracle software." Does this impact how we read David's words to Abiathar in the final scene of chapter 22? Or is it just a nice serendipity that he arrives in David's retinue armed with the ephod? Why does the narrator not reveal this crucial piece of data in chapter 22?

4. Jonathan makes an interesting cameo appearance in this episode. How does his presence serve to "encourage" David? Once more, "oath-language" is frequent in a conversation between David and Jonathan. What is your opinion on the reason why Jonathan "predicts" that David will be king, with himself as "second-in-command"? Why is *another* covenant established between the two of them? Is there any hint of self-interest here, or is this sacrificial love?

5. Saul finds an ally in the Ziphites. Do they have any discernible motives? Robert Alter (1999: 144) notes: "The motive for betraying David could equally be a desire for a reward and fear of retribution should Saul discover that they had allowed David to hide out in their territory." Are there any other options? On a different level, Saul's conversation with the Ziphites draws attention to a motif that recurs throughout this chapter: a contest of intelligence/counter-intelligence between him and David. This may help to explain Saul's rather long speech to the Ziphites. Compare Miscall's comments (1986: 143) that consider this present scene and beyond:

In 1 Sam. 26:1, the Ziphites give Saul less precise information on David's whereabouts, "and Saul rose and went down to the wilderness of Ziph." 1 Sam. 23:24-25 gives no reason to think that Saul delayed his pursuit on this occasion. However, his elaborate response does stress the themes of assurance and clarity, even though there is little reason for Saul to seek them at this time. The themes continue in the following chapters.

6. It is striking that this episode concludes with a place-name—"That is why the place is named Rock of Divisions"—since David and his men are nearly "joined" with Saul and his troops? Do you sense a providential timing in the appearance of Saul's "agent" bearing news of a Philistine incursion *just as they are closing in on David*?

CHAPTER 24

CAVING IN AND CUTTING OFF

And David went up from there and stayed at the strongholds of En-Gedi. As soon as Saul returned from following the Philistines, they reported to him, "Look, David is in the wilderness of En-Gedi!" Then Saul took 3,000 chosen men from Israel, and went to seek David and his men in the direction of the Rocks of the Wild Goats.

As he came toward some walls for sheep on the road, there was a cave there, and Saul went inside to "overshadow his feet." But David and his men were sitting in the back of the cave. Then the men of David said to him, "Look, this is the day of which the LORD said to you, 'Behold, I'm giving your enemy into your hand—do to him whatever is good in your eyes.'" And David arose and secretly cut off the wing of Saul's robe. After this, David's heart was struck, because he had cut off the wing of Saul's robe. He said to his men, "Far be it from me because of the LORD that I should do this thing against my master—the LORD's anointed—to send my hand against him, for he is the LORD's anointed!" David tore into his men with these words, and did not permit them to rise up against Saul. Then Saul arose and went onto the road.

David arose after this, and marched out of the cave. He called after Saul, saying "My lord, the king!" Saul gazed behind him, and David was prostrate, face to the ground, bowing low. David said to Saul, "Why do you listen to merely human words, saying, 'Behold,

David is seeking to harm you.' Look, this very day your eyes have seen that the LORD gave you *today* into my hand in the cave. Although some said to kill you, I looked with compassion on you, and I said, 'I won't stretch out my hand against my lord, for he is the LORD's anointed.' Now look, my father, see the wing of your robe in my hand. Since I cut off the wing of your robe and I didn't kill you, know and see that there is no evil or transgression in my hand. I haven't sinned against you, but you are hunting me down to seize my life! May the LORD judge between me and you! May the LORD take vengeance against you on my behalf, but my hand won't be against you. Just like that old proverb says, 'From the wicked, wickedness marches out'—but my hand won't be against you. Who has the king of Israel marched out after? Who are you pursuing? After a dead dog? After but a single flea? May the LORD act as a judge and make a decision between me and you. O may he see and plead my cause and grant me justice from your hand."

When David finished speaking these words to Saul, Saul said, "Is this your voice, my son David?" And Saul lifted up his voice, and he wept. He said to David, "You are more righteous than I, for you've dealt well with me, but I've dealt with you in an evil way. Today you've reported that you've acted well with me: the LORD closed me into your hand, but you didn't kill me. Now, who has *ever* found his enemy, and then let him just happily walk away? May the LORD generously repay you for the way you've treated me today. And now, look, I know that you will surely reign, and that your hand will be established over the kingdom of Israel. So now, swear an oath to me by the LORD that you won't cut off my descendants after me, or exterminate my name from my father's house." And David swore an oath to Saul. Then Saul went to his house, and David and his men went up to the stronghold.

POINTS FOR REFLECTION:

1. Reader's will notice that the "cave" in this episode has a dual function: both as a hiding place for David and his men and as a royal latrine for the king (to "overshadow the feet" is a euphemism for "lavatory discharges"). It is an incredible moment when the hunter and the hunted share the same dark space, and their paths intersect at a somewhat unlikely place. Victor Hamilton (2001: 276) observes: "That Saul and David should meet where and when and how they do in this chapter is an instance of burlesque humor or divine providence or both. Saul enters a cave to 'relieve himself' and it is the very same cave in which David and his men are hiding." Note Robert Alter's (1999: 147) comment on this passage:

> The topography is quite realistic, for the cliffs overlooking the Dead Sea in the region of En-gedi are honeycombed with caves. Power and powerlessness are precariously balanced in this episode. David and his men are in all likelihood hiding in the far end of the cave from Saul's search party. Had a contingent of soldiers entered the cave, they would have been trapped. Instead, Saul comes in alone, and he is in a double sense exposed to David and his men.

2. David's men do not appear to see the funny side of this encounter—in fact, they are very spiritually-minded, as Hamilton (2001: 276) notices: "David's allies, thankfully lacking any interest in scatological humor, suggest a theological interpretation of this bathroom improvisation incident. God has used 'nature' to deliver Saul, our enemy, into our hands." Note carefully that David's men provide a "divine quotation" to back up their plan: "Look, this is the day of which the LORD said you, 'Behold, I'm giving your enemy into your hand—do to him whatever is good in your eyes.'" What does it mean to "do whatever is good in your eyes"? Where in the

narrative is the LORD recorded as saying this? Is this an "unverifiable" quotation? While David's men are supremely confident that "God is on their side," what is the problem with their words?

3. Why does David sneak up and cut the "wing" of Saul's robe? Why then is David's conscience smitten, and whose point of view is reflected here? Consider David's speech to his men, presumably in a whisper since Saul remains in the cave. On the one hand, his words display outstanding loyalty to the king, and deep respect for the "LORD's anointed." On the other hand, is their a hint of self-interest in David's speech to his future royal court? After all, "not laying a hand on the king's anointed" can be convenient policy once he is on the throne.

4. Note carefully that David waits until Saul leaves the cave and walks "on to the road." *Then* David goes out himself and commences his speech. Thus, his audience now consists of Saul and Saul's men as well as David's men. Is David being politically expedient here?

Evaluate David's speech, which according to Fokkelman (1986: 461) is his longest in the entire narrative: "David's speech in 24:10-16 is of exceptional importance. The simplest indication of this is its length. With its 26 lines it is the longest speech that we have from David!" If Fokkelman is correct, what is the significance? Consider Polzin (1993: 210):

>...the dialogue between David and Saul in chapter 24 also betrays the self-interested motivation of both of them. On the one hand, nothing is emphasized more in this chapter than that David refused to kill Saul because he was "the LORD's anointed ... the reader cannot help realizing that the

speaker of these words is *also* the LORD's anointed.

5. Do "clothes make the man"? O. H. Prouser (1996: 27-37) observes that clothing is an important symbol in the larger David narrative. At several significant moments, clothing becomes a literary device "that highlights David's rise to power and Saul's fall from grace." Compile a list of occasions thus far in the narrative where clothing has been an important feature. Moreover, comment on other "robe moments" in the story. In this instance of chapter 24, the picture of David "holding up the piece of Saul's robe" is a powerful image, since it looks backwards (recalling Saul's ripping of Samuel's robe) and forwards (to chapter 28, and even 1 Kings 11). Consider Miscall's (1986: 148) opinion:

> We hear, but Saul sees the skirt of his robe in David's hand. The robe is a symbol of Samuel, of the kingdom, and of Saul's rejection. "She said, 'An old man is coming up and he is wrapped in a robe [me'il].' Saul *knew* that it was Samuel and he bowed with his face to the ground and paid homage" (1 Sam. 28:14). Saul is again told that "the Lord has torn the kingdom from your hand and given it to your neighbor, to David" (1 Sam. 28:17). For the first time, Samuel names Saul's successor. However, the cut or torn robe in chapter 24 is an ambiguous symbol of David's succession and success, since it points ahead to a future date when the Lord tears the kingdom from the hand of Solomon, David's son (1 Kings 11:11-13), and when another prophet from Shiloh, Ahijah will tear his new "garment" as a symbol of the rending of the kingdom from the hand of Solomon (1 Kings 11:29-31). David is uttering far more than he is aware of when he tells Saul, "See the skirt of your robe in my hand."

6. What is the literary effect of David's "proverb" that he quotes to Saul: Just like that old proverb says, 'From the wicked, wickedness marches out'—but my hand won't be against you"? Consider Robert Alter's (1999: 150) assessment: "The gnomic saying—only three words in Hebrew!—that David chooses to cite is archly double edged: Wicked acts are perpetrated only by the wicked, so I won't be the one to touch you. But there is also the distinct hint that the wicked person in question could be Saul himself. Though David cannot know this, Saul will die by his own hand." What other moments of foreshadowing occur in this chapter?

7. How does Saul's reaction to David's speech impact his characterization? Why does he ask, "Is this your voice, my son David?" Surely he knows it is David, so what is the deeper purpose of his question? In terms of the narrative chronology, not so long ago Saul is hurling his spear at David with lethal intent. Even now, he is "on the road" hunting David's life—yet he says to David "*I know that you will surely reign*"! Comment on irony of this situation. Finally, why is Saul so keen to extract an oath from David?

CHAPTER 25

A FOOL AND A WINESKIN

Samuel died, and all Israel gathered together. They lamented for him, and buried him at his house at Ramah. And David arose, and went down to the wilderness of Paran.

Now there was a man of Maon who worked in Carmel. The man was very rich, having 3,000 sheep and 1,000 goats. And he was shearing his sheep in Carmel. The man's name was Nabal, and his wife's name was Abigail. The wife had good insight and great beauty, but the husband was severe and evil in his practices, even though he was a Calebite.

In the wilderness, David heard that Nabal was shearing his sheep. And David sent 10 young lads, saying to them, "Go up to Carmel, and when you come to Nabal, ask him (on my behalf) if all is well. You'll say, 'To life! Peace be with you, your house, and everything you own. And now, I've heard that you are shearing—indeed, your shepherds have been among us; we didn't harass them, and nothing was missing the whole time they were in Carmel. Ask your lads, and they'll tell you! So may these young men find favor in your eyes, for they've come on a happy day. Give your servants whatever your hand may find, and to your son, David.'"

So David's lads came and spoke all these things to Nabal in David's name. Then they waited. And Nabal answered David's staff, and said, "Who is David? Who is the son of Jesse? Nowadays many slaves are breaking away from their bosses! So, I should take my

168

food, my water, and the meat I've slaughtered for my sheep-shearers and give it to men from who knows where?" So David's young lads turned around and went on their way. They came back and reported all these things to him. And David said to his men, "Let every man strap on his sword." So every man strapped on his sword, as did David himself, and about 400 men went up after David, while 200 remained with the equipment.

Now one of the young lads reported this to Nabal's wife Abigail, saying, "Look, David sent messengers from the wilderness to bless our boss, but he *screamed* at them. Yet the men were very good to us. They never harassed us, and nothing was missing for the whole time we were walking around with them in the open country. They were a wall for us—night and day—the whole time we were tending the flocks with them. So now, think about it and see what you should do, because evil is headed for our boss and all his household. But he's a son of Belial whenever anyone speaks to him!" Then Abigail hurried and took 200 loaves of bread, two wineskins, five dressed sheep, five measures of parched grain, 100 bunches of raisins, and 200 fig-cakes, and she loaded them on donkeys. She said to her servant lad, "Pass on ahead of me, and look, I'll be coming behind you!" (But she did not tell her husband Nabal.)

As she was riding her donkey and descending into the mountain shadows, look!, David and his men were coming down toward her, and she ran into them. Now David had said, "What a disappointment, that I guarded this guy's possessions in the wilderness—and *nothing* he owned was missing—and he treats me with evil instead of good! So may God do to David's enemies and even more if I leave alive anyone who 'urinates against the wall' by morning!" And Abigail saw David, and she quickly got down from her donkey. She fell down on her face before David and bowed low to the ground. She fell on his feet, and said, "Against me, O my lord, be the guilt! Please let your maidservant speak a word in your ear, and listen to the words of your maidservant. Don't let my lord take to heart this man of Belial, this Nabal! Indeed, just like his name, so he is: Nabal is his name and 'foolishness' is with him. But *I*, your maidservant, didn't see the young lads whom my master sent. So now, my lord, as the LORD lives and as you live—the LORD who has restrained you from blood and saved your own hand from yourself—so now may all your enemies and those who seek to do evil toward my lord be like Nabal! But let this blessing which your handmaid has brought to my lord be given to the young lads who walk in my lord's footsteps. Please forgive your maidservant's transgression. Indeed, the LORD will surely make a true house for my lord, because my lord fights the LORD's battles, and evil won't be found in you for as long as you live. Should any man arise to pursue you and seek your life, may my lord's life be bound up in the bundle of the living with the LORD your God, and may the life of your enemies be hurled forth just like the packet of the slingshot. And when the LORD fulfills every good thing he has promised to my lord and appoints you as leader of Israel, then this matter won't be a stumbling block or cause for heartache to my lord for having needlessly poured out blood, for my lord has saved himself from it! When the LORD deals well with my lord, may *you* remember your maidservant."

David said to Abigail, "Blessed be the LORD God of Israel, who has sent you to meet me today! And blessed be your good insight, and blessed be you, who has prevented me from incurring bloodshed today, and saved my hand from it! For as surely as the LORD God of Israel lives—who has restrained me from bringing evil on you—if you hadn't come to meet me, then by morning Nabal wouldn't have had anyone left who 'urinates against the wall'." Then David took from her hand that which she brought for him. He said to her, "Go up in peace to your house. See, I've listened to your voice, and I've shown partiality to you."

As Abigail returned to Nabal, look, he was hosting a feast in his house like the feast of a king! Now Nabal's heart was in good form, since he was very drunk, and she did not report anything to him, whether great or small, until the morning light. But in the morning, just as the wine was going out from Nabal, his wife reported these things to him. His heart died within him, and he became like a stone. About ten days later, the LORD struck Nabal, and he died.

Then David heard that Nabal had died, and he said, "Blessed be the LORD, who has pleaded the case of my disgrace from the hand of Nabal. He has restrained his servant from evil, but the evil of Nabal he has turned back on his own head!" Then David sent and spoke about Abigail, in order to secure her for a wife. And David's staff came to Abigail at Carmel, and they spoke to her, saying, "David sent us to you in order to secure you as a wife." She arose, and bowed low, face to the ground. She said, "Look, your maidservant is a hired-hand to wash the feet of my lord's staff." Abigail quickly arose and mounted her donkey, with five servant girls walking beside her. She followed after David's messengers, and she became his wife.

Now David had taken Ahinoam from Jezreel, and so both of them, the two of them, became his wives. But Saul had given his daughter Michal, the wife of David, to Palti son of Laish, who was from Gallim.

POINTS FOR REFLECTION:

1. What is the significance that this episode of chapter 25 begins with the "death notice" of the prophet Samuel? Is it significant that *immeadiately after* Saul says to David "you will surely reign" at the end of chapter 24, Samuel (the kingmaker) dies? Is there a smooth transition between the prophet's funeral and David's wandering in

the wilderness of Paran? As the chapter continues, carefully note how Nabal and Abigail are described. Keep this general principle in mind: when a certain detail of someone's personality is given the narrative, chances are very good that such a quality will be germane to the events of the story. Hence, when we read, "the woman had good insight and great beauty, but the man was severe and evil in his practices," one expects that these various qualities will emerge as the story progresses. Incidentally, the name "Nabal" means both "fool" and "wineskin." Moreover, Nabal is a "Calebite," a Hebrew term that also means "dog." This is the same term that David uses earlier when he asks, "Who are you pursuing? After a *dead dog*?" Ironically, Nabal concludes this chapter as a "dead dog," so there may be a certain grim humor here.

2. The small detail of David's men "waiting" after they deliver David's long greeting to Nabal is perhaps indicative of how they will be treated. Is there anything *political* in Nabal's words? Does he know about the David-Saul estrangement, and is he acting in a pro-Saul manner? Recall that Saul has been to Carmel before, as Samuel is told in chapter 15, "Saul has arrived at Carmel, and look, he is erecting a monument for himself." So, the reader wonders if Nabal is being intentionally contemptuous of David when he says, "lots of slaves are running away these days . . ."

3. Comment on David's violent reaction as his agents return. If one grants that Nabal's response is foolish, does this justify David's "sword-strapping"? Does the (intended) punishment fit the crime? Is this somewhat excessive, or expected in the circumstances? How does this reaction characterize David?

4. The servant's report to Abigail is gushy with praise for David's men, while incriminating against Nabal (replete with the epithet,

"son of Belial," which is seen previously in the narrative, including the sons of Eli in chapter 2). Abigail's intervention illustrates that she indeed possesses the "good insight" disclosed earlier by the narrator. On another level, though, this is not the first time that a married woman will enter David's life (see 2 Samuel 11), and her *very* long speech is extraordinary. First, she predicts David's future "leadership" of Israel. Some commentators have wondered if she is positioning herself *just in case* she happens to become a widow. Is this plausible? If not, then what does she mean by this statement: "When the LORD deals well with my lord, may *you* remember your maidservant"? Second, does her reference to a "slingshot" allude to the Goliath episode? If so, does she intend it as flattery? Evaluate David's response to the very long speech of this beautiful wife.

5. The timing of Abigail's report to Nabal is remarkable. She declines to tell him when he is "drunk" (in the midst of his "royal feast'), but instead waits until the morning. According to a recent article by Peter Leithart (2001: 525-27), Abigail gives her report to Nabal "*just as the wine is leaving him*"! Admittedly, this is a rather crude translation for a rather crude fellow, and something of a poetic justice since his name also means "wineskin." So, both chapter 24 and chapter 25 have David's "opponents" responding to "the call of nature" at critical moments in the story. Further, there is a rather vulgar irony: David declares that no one who "urinates against the wall" (i.e., a male, perhaps "one who waters the feet") belonging to Nabal shall be alive by morning, and as it turns out, "in the morning, just as the wine is leaving Nabal ('wineskin')," he turns into a stone.

6. After a rather brief courtship, David and Abigail are united in matrimony. Are there any objections to Abigail becoming David's wife? Why does chapter 25 conclude with a recitation of David's

wives? Note carefully the narration here: "Now David had taken Ahinoam from Jezreel, and so both of them, the two of them, became his wives." What does this communicate to the reader? Is the reader invited to consider David's treatment of women? Is "Ahinoam" the same name as Saul's wife? Finally, what about the "Michal" factor? Doesn't she "love" David? Why would Saul give her to Palti?

CHAPTER 26

CAMPSITE DISCOURSE

Then the Ziphites came to Saul at Gibeah, saying, "Isn't David hiding himself in Hachilah Hill facing Jeshimon?" And Saul arose and went down to the wilderness of Ziph, along with 3000 chosen men of Israel, to seek David in the wilderness of Ziph. Saul camped near Hachilah Hill facing Jeshimon. But David was staying in the wilderness, and he saw that Saul had come after him into the wilderness. Then David sent out spies, and confirmed that indeed Saul had arrived. And David arose and came to the place where Saul was camped. David saw the place where Saul was lying down, near Abner son of Ner, commander of his army. (Now Saul was lying down in the trench, with the troops encamped all around him.)

Then David addressed Ahimelech the Hittite and Abishai son of Zeruiah, Joab's brother, and said, "Who will go down with me to Saul, to the camp?" Abishai said, "I'll go down with you." So David and Abishai came to the army at night, and look, Saul was laying down, sleeping in the trench. His spear was thrust into the ground near his head, with Abner and the troops lying all around him. And Abishai said to David, "Today God has closed your enemy right into your hand! So now, let me strike him with the spear right to the ground with one stroke and I won't need a second!" David said to Abishai, "Don't destroy him, for who can send his hand against the LORD's anointed and be innocent?" And David said, "As the LORD lives, the LORD himself will strike him, or his day will come and he'll die, or he'll go down into battle and be swept away. Far be it from me by the LORD that I should send my hand against the LORD's anointed! So now, take the spear by his head and the water-jug, and let's go."

Then David took the spear and water-jug near Saul's head, and they left. Nobody saw, no one knew, and no one woke up. All of them were asleep, for the LORD had caused a deep sleep to fall on them. And David crossed over to the opposite side. He stood on a hilltop some distance away, with a wide space between them. Then David called out to the troops and Abner, son of Ner, saying, "Won't you answer Abner?" Abner answered, and said, "Who are you that calls to the king?" David said to Abner, "Aren't you a man? Who in Israel is like you? Why didn't you guard your master, the king? Indeed, one of the troops came to destroy your master, the king! This thing you've done is not good—as the LORD lives, you're all sons of death because you all failed to keep watch over your master, the LORD's anointed! So now, look around! Where are the king's spear and the water-jug that were beside his head?"

Saul recognized David's voice, and said, "Is this your voice, my son David?" David said, "It's my voice, my master, the king." He said, "Why is my master pursuing after his servant? What have I done? What evil is on my hands? So now, please let the king listen to the words of his servant. If the LORD has incited you against me, then may he catch scent of an offering. But if this is from men, then may they be cursed before the LORD, for today they've banished me from attachment to the LORD's inheritance, saying, 'Go, serve other gods!' So now, don't let my blood fall to the ground outside of the LORD's presence. Indeed, the king has marched out to seek but a single flea, just like someone would chase after a partridge on the hills!"

Saul said, "I've sinned. Return, David my son, I won't harm you again—as it stands, my life was precious in your eyes on this day. Look, I've been a fool, and I've erred grievously." David answered, and said, "Look, the king's spear! Send over one of the young lads to fetch it. The LORD will return to every man his righteous acts and faithful service—the LORD gave you into my hand today, but I was unwilling to send my hand against the LORD's anointed. So behold, just as your life was important in my eyes today, thus may my life be important in the eyes of the LORD, such that he rescues me from every distress!" Saul said to David, "May you be blessed, David my son. Surely you'll do many things, and certainly prevail." Then David went on his way, and Saul returned to his place.

POINTS FOR REFLECTION:

1. There are a number of ways in which chapters 24 and 26 can be compared and contrasted. Most obviously, in both episodes David has a "chance" to strike Saul, yet declines. In chapter 24, Saul arrived in the cave by "coincidence." In chapter 26, David seems more calculated, as Miscall (1986: 158) notes: "This is no chance encounter at Hachilah, as it was at Engedi. David 'saw that Saul had come after him into the wilderness; David sent spies, and he knew that Saul had come.' David's approach and view are described in the detail befitting a careful plan." Compare Alter's (1999: 162) comment: "this story will prove to be an *inversion* of the earlier one, David discovering Saul instead of the other way around." So, after David determines that Saul has indeed come after him, does he carefully plan his encounter with Saul? Is it his visual perspective that is provided when the reader is confronted with the following: "So David and Abishai came to the army at night, *and look, Saul was laying down, sleeping in the trench. His spear was thrust into the ground near his head, with Abner and the troops lying all around him*"?

177

Ironically, the "spear of Saul" usually foreshadows danger to someone else, but on this occasion the threat of the "spear" is on Saul personally.

2. It is a significant moment in the episode when David speaks to Ahimelech the Hittite and Abishai son of Zeruiah. First, Ahimelech the Hittite does not turn up again in the story, while this moment serves to introduce a very important family for the rest of 2 Samuel: the sons of Zeruiah (David's sister!). That Abishai is the volunteer instead of Ahimelech is important. Is David glad that Abishai makes the decision? There is a nice symmetry between Abishai and Abner in this episode, and since these two will become adversaries in 2 Samuel, this introduction merits reflection. Consider Miscall's (1986: 158) comment:

> The parallel between them [Abishai and Abner] is interesting—both are generals in their respective armies, and both drop suddenly from the narrative to reappear in 2 Samuel. Abishai volunteers to go with David to the camp. Why does David want an accomplice and only one at that? David may want someone, especially a man like Abishai, to go down to Saul's camp with him to serve as his "straight man" by proposing to kill Saul on the spot.

Abishai, Joab's brother, reveals himself as one who is not particularly alert to the subtleties of "interpreting David." His proposal to strike Saul mirrors the words of David's men (including Abishai?) in the cave of En-gedi in chapter 24. And again, David's words underscore "the LORD's anointed" with pointed effect. Is it somewhat humorous that David *himself* fetches the king's spear, presumably the same weapon that was previously aimed at his own head? How should the reader interpret the "deep sleep from the LORD" that falls on the troops?

3. Why does David choose to address Abner first? Is Abner a dangerous rival? Note Abner again responds to a question without a definitive rejoinder, just like his first piece of dialogue with Saul in chapter 17. Once more, David highlights his respect for "the LORD's anointed." As with chapter 24, is there any hint of self-interest here? Some commentators have pointed out that since David has been anointed as the next king, this would certainly be an attractive policy.

4. Some exegetes have struggled with a strange image, as David compares Saul's pursuit to someone hunting for a "partridge on the hills." However, J. P. Fokkelman (1986: 546) notices that there is a neat little wordplay here: "partridge" (קרא) forms a pun with "caller" (קרא), with the implication that Saul is pursuing a bird in the mountains, but the bird is now perched "on the hill" and "calling" out to the king! On a deeper level, comment on David's theological language here. To this point in the narrative, David has distinguished himself as someone who is highly adept with words, and creates vivid faith-pictures through his use of language. He bravely invokes divine involvement at many points on the journey. This is something to bear in mind, since later in the story (e.g., after the events of 2 Samuel 11) David's theological language undergoes something of a shift. David's spiritual utterances, then, become something of an index to his ongoing characterization.

5. Saul's response is more equivocal than chapter 24, where he predicts that David will "reign." However, Saul does predict "great things" for David here, and as Robert Alter observes, these "words of fatherly blessing are the last ones Saul speaks to David: the two never meet again" (1999: 167). Is it a sad moment as Saul's final

words to his (former?) son-in-law are words of benediction and assurance of success? Or is the irony well-deserved in light of Saul's irrational pursuit of David, who has twice spared his life?

CHAPTER 27

RESIDING WITH A PHILISTINE POTENTATE

And David said in his heart, "Now one of these days I'm going to be swept away by Saul's hand. There's nothing better for me to do than slip away to the land of the Philistines—Saul will despair of continually seeking me within the borders of Israel, and I'll slip out of his grasp." Then David arose with his 600 men with him, and crossed over to Achish son of Maoch, king of Gath. So David stayed with Achish in Gath (along with all of his men and their households, plus David and his two wives: Ahinoam of Jezreel and Abigail, wife of Nabal of Carmel). Saul received the report that David had fled to Gath, and he no longer searched for him.

And David said to Achish, "If I've found favor in your eyes, then give me a place in one of the country towns and I'll live there. Why should your servant live in the royal city with you?" So that very day Achish gave him Ziklag (and ever since then Ziklag has belonged to the kings of Judah, until now).

The length of time that David stayed in Philistine territory was one year and four months. David and his men went up and raided the Geshurites, the Girzites, and the Amalekites (since these were the inhabitants of the land from ancient times) until you reach Shur, right up to the land of Egypt. David would strike the land, and would not leave any man or woman alive. He would take flocks, cattle, donkeys, camels, and clothing, and then return and go to

Achish. Achish would say, "Where did you raid today?" David would say, "The Negeb of Judah," or "The Negeb of Jerahmeel," or "The Negeb of the Kenites." (But David would not leave any man or woman alive in case they returned to Gath: "Lest they report on us, saying, 'This is what David has done, and such is his usual practice!'" This was his *modus operandi* for the entire time he lived in Philistine territory.)

And Achish believed David, saying, "Surely he has become utterly odious among his own people in Israel, and he'll be my slave forever!"

POINTS FOR REFLECTION:

1. David's inner thoughts seem to reveal his doubt over Saul's resolve. Why does he choose to journey to Achish, king of Gath, again? On the last occasion David was in Gath, Achish's staff had serious concerns, and David feigns madness because of his fear. Yet now he travels once more to Gath, this time with a sizable entourage! Observe the subtle mention of Abigail as the *"wife* of Nabal." Some translations render the Hebrew term as "widow," but it seems preferable to opt for "wife." Note that later in the narrative (2 Samuel 12) Bathsheba is referred to as "the wife of Uriah" even after Uriah is dead and *after* she and David are married. Is this a subtle indictment?

2. Miscall observes that David has quite a long sojourn in Gath, and further, that Saul gives up the pursuit (1986: 163-4): "But why does Saul give up the chase? Does he consider David to be out of reach in Philistia, or does he think that David has deserted and gone over to the Philistines for good? Does David know that Saul has given up?" Are David's words to Achish duplicitous? What does he

mean when he says, "Why should your servant live in the royal city with you?" Will David "do anything" to survive? How does this reflect on his characterization?

3. What hints are there in this chapter about David's royalty? Note carefully that Achish gives David the city of Ziklag, which Alter (1999: 169) notes is significant: "This seemingly technical geopolitical notice serves a function of historical foreshadowing, as Fokkelman observes: David, the Philistine vassal and fugitive from Saul, is destined to found a lasting dynasty, 'the kings of Judah.'"

4. David's raiding sorties are directed at non-Israelite settlements. What is revealed here? Some commentators have struggled with (at least) two ethical issues in this chapter. First, how should a reader evaluate David's carnage, the large-scale annihilation of villages? What about his acquisition of assets through (potentially) dubious means? Is this legitimate, or ethically problematic? Second, how should a reader understand David's "lie" to Achish, in response to Achish's query about "where" David went raiding?

5. The chapter has a nice envelope structure: it commences with David's inner thoughts, and concludes with an interior glimpse of Achish. How is the king of Gath presented on this narrative canvas? Why is he so keen to secure David as a "slave"? What about the issue of David's "previous history" of madness? Did Achish sense that David was dissembling in chapter 21? Evaluate Miscall's comment (1986:165-6):

> Is Achish stupid or gullible; is David an extremely capable confidence man? What of the booty from the raids? If Achish is receiving large amounts of booty from David, is he then blinded, perhaps knowingly, by it? Achish may share with

Nabal's men a self-interested involvement with David. On the other hand, like Nabal, Achish seriously underestimates David by regarding him as a servant or slave. David serves Achish for his own present interests or future plans, not because he is Achish's servant, let alone "a servant forever." This is analogous to a major thread of my reading of the relationship between Saul and David. Saul may be obsessed with his pursuit of David and may gravely overstep his authority, as in the massacre of Nob, but whom is he pursuing? Is this one of the king's "faithful servants" (1 Sam. 22:14) and loyal general of his army? Or is this a cunning and unscrupulous rival whose hand will not be against the king, but neither will it be with the king in his hour of need? Achish errs when he considers David a permanent servant; does Saul err when he considers David a permanent enemy? (cf. 1 Sam. 18:29)?

CHAPTER 28

THE MEDIUM AND THE MESSAGE

At that time the Philistines assembled their camp for war, to battle against Israel. And Achish said to David, "Naturally you know you'll march out to the camp with me—you and your men." David said to Achish, "Therefore you'll know what your servant can do!" Achish said to David, "Therefore I'm appointing you as *the keeper of my head* forever!"

(Now Samuel had died, and all Israel had mourned for him and buried him in his hometown of Ramah. But Saul had driven out the necromancers and mediums from the land.)

Then the Philistines arrived and assembled themselves, and established their camp at Shunem. And Saul gathered all Israel and camped at Gilboa. When Saul saw the Philistine camp, he was afraid, and his heart was beating rapidly. And Saul inquired of the LORD, but the LORD did not answer him, whether by dream, by Urim, or through the prophets.

Then Saul said to his servants, "Find for me a woman who is a medium, so that I can go to her, and inquire of her." His servants said to him, "Look, there's a woman who is a medium in En-Dor." So Saul disguised himself, and clothed himself in other garments. Along with two men, he went and came to the woman at night. He said, "Please summon a spirit for me, and bring up for me whoever I tell you." The woman said to him, "Look, you're *fully* aware of what Saul has done: he's cut off all the necromancers and mediums from the land! Why would you set a trap for my life, that will result in my death?" Saul swore an oath to her by the LORD, saying, "As the LORD lives, guilt will not be imputed to you in this matter." The woman said, "Who will I bring up for you?" He said, "Bring up Samuel for me." And the woman saw Samuel, and cried out in a great voice. The woman said to Saul, "Why have you deceived me? You are Saul!" The king said to her, "Don't be afraid. What do you see?" The woman said to Saul, "I see gods rising from the earth." He said to her, "What is his appearance?" She said, "An old man is rising up, and he's wrapped in a robe." And Saul knew that it was Samuel, and he was prostrate with his face to the ground, and bowed low. Samuel said to Saul, "Why have you agitated me by bringing me up?" Saul said, "I'm under great stress! The Philistines are battling against me, and God has turned away from me. He won't answer me, whether by the hand of the prophets or through dreams, so I'm calling on you to cause me to know what I must do."

Samuel said, "Why are you asking me? The LORD has turned away from you, and become your enemy. The LORD has done to you exactly as he spoke by my hand: the LORD has ripped the kingdom from your hand, and given it to your friend, *to David*. Because you didn't listen to the voice of the LORD, and didn't execute his fierce wrath against Amalek, therefore the LORD has done this thing to you today. The LORD will give Israel, along with you, into the hand of the Philistines, and tomorrow you and your sons will be with me, and the LORD will give the entire camp of Israel into Philistine hands."

Instantaneously Saul fell down, to the fullness of his height, on the ground, and he was very afraid of Samuel's words. Moreover, there was no strength left in him, for he had not eaten anything all that day or night. Then the woman came to Saul, and she saw that he was greatly disturbed, and she said to him, "Look, your maidservant listened to your voice, and I took my life in my hands and I listened to the words you said to me. So now, please, you must listen to your maidservant's voice, and I'll set before you a little bit of bread. Eat, and then there will be strength in you so you can go on the journey." He refused, and said, "I won't eat." But his servants tried to break through to him, as did the woman, and he listened to them. He arose from the ground, and sat on the bed. Now the woman had a fattened calf in the house. She hurried, and slaughtered it, and took flour, kneaded it, and baked unleavened bread. Then she brought it before Saul and his servants, and they ate. And they arose, and they went away on that night.

POINTS FOR REFLECTION:

1. It seems that both Achish and David are doing some posturing as war is mounting between Israel and the Philistines. Why does Achish inform David that he will have to fight against Israel *if* David has been continually making raids for the last year? Does he not "believe" David (as is claimed in the previous chapter)? What about David's response? Is he being equivocal? Note the unconscious irony in Achish's words, "Therefore I'm appointing you as *the keeper of my head* forever!" Some translations render this expression as "my bodyguard," but the irony lies in the fact that David previously held in his hands "the head" of another leading citizen of Gath, Goliath!

2. Why does the narrator repeat the "death notice" of Samuel, since this issue has been buried long ago in chapter 25? Furthermore, what is Saul's motive for expelling the witches and the sorcerers? Is he acting in accordance with the Torah, or is he concerned with any "rival" gaining access to supernatural guidance? Saul is on the threshold of transgressing his own moratorium.

187

3. Notice Saul "asks" again, yet his asking fails. Why does the LORD not answer Saul? Why is Saul so concerned with divine inquiry, and why is the LORD silent? Comment on Saul's use of a "disguise." Is this effective? In light of the fact that he is "head and shoulders" taller than everyone else in Israel, how on earth can he be functionally disguised? Is there anything symbolic here? Barbara Green (2003: 107) asks, "From whom is Saul disguising himself?" What is the significance of this episode taking place "at night"? Robert Polzin observes that Saul often does things under the cover of night. List the various places where Saul is active during the nocturnal hours, and how this *temporal* component affects his characterization.

4. Some commentators have suggested that the medium is suspicious of these late-night visitors. If so, could the physical stature of her guest play a part here? Alternatively, are her words unconsciously ironic? Notice that Saul reassures her by swearing an oath "by the LORD." Is this somewhat paradoxical in light of the LORD "not answering" Saul? Why is Saul so keen to communicate with Samuel? Hitherto, Samuel has not been a harbinger of good news or a dispenser of practical advice to Saul. What might Saul expect here?

5. The details of the seance are scant. Why? Is the medium deliberately vague when she says, "I see gods rising from the earth"? Again, Barbara Green (2003: 108) asks, "How does the prophet's presence give away the king's identity? How do the powers the woman taps help her see more deeply past disguises into identities?" After Saul inquires as to the "outline" of what the woman sees, he is informed about the relative age of the man, but perhaps most poignantly, that he is "wrapped in a robe." Is this robe "ripped"? The reader must recall that the "robe" has marked Samuel

from an early point in his career, as his mother Hannah would make him a "little robe" every year. Most memorably, Saul "rips" Samuel's robe in chapter 15, which the prophet transforms into a dramatic illustration of Saul's loss of the kingdom. Does it seem somewhat incongruous that the LORD does not answer Saul, yet Samuel "appears" having died quite some time ago?

6. Describe how Samuel is presented in this scene. How do his opening words to Saul come across? Would a reader expect Saul to receive a warmer reception? What would Samuel be expected to say? What does he mean when he inquires, "Why have you agitated me by bringing me up?" Notice that his second question to Saul involves the now-familiar wordplay on Saul's name, "ask": "Samuel said, 'Why are you *asking* me?'" As Samuel speaks with King Saul, comment on how you perceive the tone of his words. Is the prophet smug? If so, does he have a right to be? Or is he speaking more benevolently to the fearful king? According to the prophet, is it "Saul's own fault" that he is in this mess? What are the reasons Samuel provides for Saul's plight? Are Samuel's words "tomorrow you and your sons will be with me" designed to be comforting to Saul?

7. As the medium of En-Dor sees Saul prostrate on the ground, "to the fullness of his height," evaluate her words to the king. Is she a wicked witch? Compare her speech with the prophet; is there a deliberate contrast, or is she simply acting out of self-preservation? After all, she is guilty of a serious legal violation. But is it not possible to construe the woman as having mercy on Saul, as she serves him his "last meal" with some dignity? Comment on Saul's presentation here, in light of both the prophet's words and the witch's aftercare.

8. At the end of this dark night in chapter 28, how then should Samuel the prophet be read in light of the entire narrative, from his birth until (beyond) the grave? At the outset of this study, it is suggested that as a literary character the prophet is underestimated and under-read. It is too easy to simply assert "he is a prophet, and therefore infallible." Could it be that the biblical writer causes the reader to reflect on the difficult role of the prophetic office in this new era of the monarchy? Could it be that a central purpose of 1 Samuel is to advise "future leaders" to constantly be alert to their own agendas? On the other hand, is a more critical reading of Samuel ill-advised? Alter's (1999: xv) analysis is worth quoting at length, and merits a careful response:

> Samuel is a densely imagined character, and, it must be said, in many respects a rather unattractive one. ... The prophet Samuel may have God on his side, but he is also an implacable, irascible man, and often a palpably self-interested one as well. His resistance to the establishment of the monarchy may express a commitment to the noble idea of the direct kingship of God over Israel, but it is also motivated by resentment that he must surrender authority, and the second of his two antimonarchic speeches [chapter 12] is informed by belligerent self-defensiveness about his own career as national leader. When he chooses Saul, he wants to play him as his puppet, dictating elaborate scenarios to the neophyte king, even setting him up for failure by arriving at an arranged rendezvous at the last possible moment. He is proud, imperious, histrionic—until the very end, when he is conjured up by Saul as a ghost on the eve of the fatal battle at Mount Gilboa.

It would be misleading, I think, to imagine that any of this is intended to discredit the idea of prophetic authority. Samuel is invested with prophetic power by an act of God. But the writer understands that he is also a man, all too human, and that any kind of power, including spiritual power, can lead to abuse. Samuel toys with the idea of creating a kind of prophetic dynasty through his two sons, even though they are just as corrupt as the two sons of Eli, whose immoral behavior seals the doom of their father's priestly line. ... [Does Samuel always] act with divinely authorized prophetic rightness, or, as Martin Buber thought, [does Samuel occasionally confuse] his own human impulses with God's will? The story of Samuel, then, far from being a simple promotion of prophetic ideology, enormously complicates the notion of prophecy by concretely imagining what may become of the imperfect stuff of humanity when the mantle of prophecy is cast over it.

CHAPTER 29

INTERPRETING THE LYRICS
OF *THAT* POP SONG

The Philistines assembled their entire camp at Aphek, while Israel camped at the Spring of Jezreel. The Philistine dictators were passing through in their divisions of hundreds and thousands, while David and his men were passing through at the back with Achish. And the Philistine captains said, "What's with these Hebrews?" Achish said to the Philistine captains, "Isn't this *David*, servant of Saul, king of Israel, who has been with me these days, and years? I haven't found anything against him from the day he fell in with me until today!"

But the Philistine commanders were furious with him, and said to him, "Send the man back, and let him stay in the place you assigned him! He will *not* come down with us in battle, and he will *not* be an adversary against us in battle! How can he regain his master's favor? Will it not be by the heads of these men? Isn't this *David*, who they sing to each other about in their dances, saying, 'Saul has struck his thousands, David his ten thousands'?" Then Achish drew near to David, and said to him, "As the LORD lives, you've been upright, and good *in my eyes* is your marching out and coming in with me in the camp, and I haven't found any evil in you from the day you stepped in with me until now. However, in the eyes of the dictators, you aren't good. So now, turn back, and go in peace. Don't do anything evil in the eyes of the Philistine dictators."

David said to Achish, "What have I done? What have you found in your servant from the day I came before you until now, that I can't go out and fight against the enemies of my lord the king?"

Achish answered, and said to David, "I know that you've been as good in my eyes as an angel of God. Nevertheless, the Philistine captains have said, 'He will *not* go up with us in battle.' So now, get up early in the morning—you and your lord's servants who came with you. When you've risen early in the morning and it becomes light for you, then go."

So David rose early, he and his men, in order to depart in the morning, to return to Philistine territory. Then the Philistines went up to Jezreel.

POINTS FOR REFLECTION:

1. As the Philistine battle ranks are being drawn, David is marching at the rear as the "bodyguard" (or "head-keeper") of the king of Gath. What does David intend to do once the battle commences? Are the Philistine commanders correct in their assessment of David's motives? Evaluate Herbert Kupferberg's comment on David's larger presentation in this complex narrative: "The King David who emerges from these pages is a masterful (and sometimes cunning) politician, a bold (and often opportunistic) warrior and a devoted (but also vindictive) ruler—the surprising human centerpiece of an ancient story few modern novelists can match for sheer drama."

2. Assess the dialogue between David and Achish. Is it odd that Achish, a Philistine king, swears an oath in the name of "the Lord"? If Achish was previously at odds with his own personnel in chapter 21, he seems deferential to the dictators here in chapter 29.

Comment on David's response, "What have I done? What have you found in your servant from the day I came before you until now, that I can't go out and fight against the enemies of my lord the king?" Is he for real, or is this politically-correct behavior? Who exactly are "the enemies of my lord the king," as David puts it? Or from Achish's perspective, who is "your lord" when Achish says, "So now, get up early in the morning—you and *your lord's* servants who came with you." Is it he himself (Achish), or King Saul of Israel? Would David really have fought against Saul (the LORD's anointed) and Israel, or is this a ruse?

3. J. P. Fokkelman (1986: 577) has several useful insights about the dialogue between Achish and David, and how it connects with the complaint of the Philistine leaders moments earlier. When the Philistine leaders affirm "he will *not* be an adversary against us in battle," the term "adversary" is literally "satan." Fokkelman notes that Achish then provides a contrast: the leaders complain that David will be a "satan," yet Achisch calls David an "angel":

> Achish, who is to some extent threatened by this vigorous protest [of David], first decides to reduce the pressure. He again devotes a line to praise: "I *know* that you are good in my eyes, like an angel!" His "I know" is soothing and reminiscent of a gesture of charm in the face of David's anger. He follows it with a beautiful simile: he has now dredged up something extra nice from his stock of diplomatic pleasantries and rhetorical ornaments and compares David with "a messenger of God". This apex of flattery ... is a counterpoint [to the accusation of the Philistine leaders]. The opposition is a good find by the narrator and is the most colourful in the story. Since we are now concerned with rhetoric, I

194

would take the liberty of concentrating the issue of the Philistine debate somewhat: David is a devil, says one of the parties: no, he is an angel, says the other.

4. As the chapter draws to a close, is there an intentional structural contrast between "the night" of chapter 28 and "the morning light" of chapter 29? Respond to Peter Miscall's (1986: 176-77) various questions:

> Emphasis is on departure at morning's first light. Does David's departure coincide with Saul's departure from Endor? ... Chapter 29 is a "typical chapter" in view of [its] forcing of a rereading and in view of its detail, repetition, and ambiguity. What of Achish and his perception of David? What of David and his perception of Achish, Saul, his own future, and the coming battle at Mt. Gilboa? What of the whole chapter? Why this lengthy presentation of David with the Philistines at this point? From one perspective, the ambi-guity and equivocation of the living characters, especially Achish and David, underscore the failed certitude of the dead in chapter 28. Saul will die, and David will be king, but why is not certain, particularly in regard to the word and doings of the Lord. Does Saul die because of divine judg-ment, because of his own failures and weaknesses as leader and general, or because the Philistines fight courageously and valiantly?

CHAPTER 30

"LEFT BEHIND"

David and his men arrived in Ziklag on the third day, but the Amalekites had raided the south, including Ziklag. They struck Ziklag, and burned it with fire. They took the women as captives, from the least to the greatest. They put no one to death, but led them off and went on their way.

Then David and his men came to the city, but look, it was burning with fire, and their wives and sons and daughters had been taken captive! David and his men with him lifted up their voices, and they wept, until they no longer had any strength left to weep. (David's two wives had been taken captive: Ahinoam of Jezreel and Abigail, wife of Nabal the Carmelite.) David was in great distress, for the people were talking about stoning him, for everyone was bitter of soul over their sons and daughters, but David strengthened himself in the LORD his God.

And David said to Abiathar the priest, son of Ahimelech, "Bring me, please, the ephod." So Abiathar brought the ephod to David. Then David asked the LORD, saying, "Should I pursue after this band of pirates? Will I overtake it?" He said to him, "Pursue, for you will surely overtake, and you will indeed rescue!" So David left with 600 of his men. They came to the Besor River, where those who were going to be left behind halted. David and 400 men continued the pursuit, but 200 men halted, who were too exhausted to cross over the Besor River.

Then they found an Egyptian man in the open country, and brought him to David. They gave him some bread to eat, and supplied him with water to drink. Then they gave him a slice of fig cake and two bunches of raisins. He ate, and his spirit was restored, for he had not eaten anything or drank any water for three days and three nights. And David said to him, "Who do you belong to, and where are you from?" The Egyptian servant lad said, "I'm a slave that belongs to an Amalekite, but my master abandoned me when I got sick three days ago. We were raiding south of the Cherethites toward Judah and south of Caleb, and we torched Ziklag with fire." David said to him, "Can you bring me down to these pirates?" He said, "Swear an oath by God to me that you won't kill me or hand me over to my master, and I'll bring you down to the pirates."

So he brought them down, and look, they were abandoned all over the face of the earth, eating, drinking, and partying with all the great plunder that they had taken from the land of the Philistines and Judah! Then David struck them from twilight until the evening of the next day. None escaped, with the exception of 400 young lads who rode off on camels and fled. So David rescued all which Amalek had taken, and David rescued his two wives. Nothing was missing—either small or large, or sons and daughters—from the spoil they had taken for themselves, and David recovered it all. David took all the sheep and cattle, which they drove ahead of that herd, and they said, "This is David's plunder!"

Then David came to the 200 men who were too exhausted to walk after David, and were left at the Besor River. As they came out to meet David and the people with him, David drew near to the group and asked if they were well. However, all the evil and "Belial" men of David's company who had gone out with him spoke up, and said, "Because they didn't go up with us, none of the plunder we rescued should be given to them. But every man can lead away his wife and kids, and go." David said, "This won't happen, my

197

brothers, with that which the LORD has given to us. For he has watched over us, and given the pirates who came against us into our hand. Who should listen to you on this issue? The share of the one who goes down to battle will be the same as the one who is left behind with the supplies—they *will* share alike!" So from that day onward it was established as a statute and a judgment for Israel, right up until now.

Then David came to Ziklag and sent portions of the plunder to the elders of Judah, his neighbors, saying, "Look, a blessing from the plunder of the LORD's enemies." It was for those in Bethel, South Ramath, Jattir, Aroer, Siphmoth, Eshtemoa, Racal, the cities of the Jerahmeelites, the cities of the Kenites, Hormah, Bor-Ashan, Athach, Hebron, and all the places where David and his men had walked around.

POINTS FOR REFLECTION:

1. Is there something of an irony in the fact that in chapter 28 Samuel declares that Saul is a failure because of "the Amalekite affair" (see chapter 15), and now here in chapter 30 the Amalekites plunder David? In chapter 27 David plunders the Amalekites; now they "plunder" David. Fokkelman (1986: 579) suggests that the Amalekite raid on David and capture of his wives could be "revenge," as the Amalekites "threaten to inflict a disaster and deep humiliation on David." Is this plausible?

2. What does this clause mean: "but David strengthened himself in the LORD his God"? Could there be something of a contrast between Saul and David here, since both are respectively "under stress" (צרר) in chapters 28 and 30? (See further Hamilton 2001: 285; Brueggemann 1990: 201.) Comment on the repeated fact that

David inquires of God and is given a loquacious response, whereas Saul "asks" and is only given the sounds of silence.

3. If David is "under stress" because of the missing wives and children—notwithstanding the positive oracle—the report that 200 of his men are "too exhausted" to continue the chase is probably not welcome news. Hence, the discovery of the abandoned Egyptian slave must be something of a relief, although the infirmity of the slave represents a considerable obstacle. Fokkelman (1986: 583) notes that the first meal is not altogether successful, as the Egyptian slave only recovers *after* "he has been revived with cakes of fruit of high food value," and thus by this means "the narrator shows how deplorable the slave's condition was." What does this augur for the Amalekites' treatment of the wives and children of David and his men? Moreover, is the "weakness" of David's 200 men (who are too tired to pursue after their wives and children) similar to the "weakness" of the Egyptian? Evaluate Miscall's (1985: 179) comments:

> He [David] leaves in such haste that 200 of his men are too tired to continue the chase; these are not similar to the 200 he had, on another occasion, left with the baggage (1 Sam. 25:13). The theme of weakness appears again here and in vv. 11-15; the Egyptian lad is weak because he has not eaten or drunk for three days. The detail of the food and drink emphasizes David's straits; the lad, who must first be well fed, is his only hope of ever locating "this band." The lad replies to David's demand in familiar terms—swear, kill, deliver. At first encounter, even a young Egyptian lad fears David and enters into an explicit relation of mutual self-interest with David. "Swear to me by God that you will not kill me or hand me over [*sagar*] to my master, and I will

bring you down to this band" (v. 15). There is poignancy to his speech, since it intones both Saul's earlier request for an oath from David not to kill him (1 Sam. 24:22) and Saul's death on Mt. Gilboa. Previously Saul had been hungry and weak from not eating.

4. The recovery of the families and livestock illustrates David's military skill, and underscores the highly favorable divine oracle earlier in the chapter. But equally important is the political skill by which David resolves the discord in the camp over the plunder. David's political skill is evident in at least three ways here. First, note the subtle description of the men who previously were "too exhausted" are now referred to by David as those "left behind with the supplies." Since these 200 men were presumably among those who wanted to "stone" David earlier, his magnanimity appears in a highly favorable light. Second, the distribution of "the blessing" to the various towns and elders of Judah anticipates David's rise to power in Judah, and of course he is shortly to be crowned king of Judah in Hebron. This distribution illustrates David's *own awareness* of his growing power. Thus, "the story that began with deprivation ... is now completed by the wealth that David spreads over South Judah" (Fokkelman 1986: 591). Finally, some commentators suggest that these events in chapter 30 are occurring *simultaneously* with the events of chapter 31. If this is possible, then while David is distributing this wealth around his home tribe of Judah, Saul is "falling" on the slopes of Mount Gilboa. Respond to Polzin's (1993: 223) analysis of this scene:

> All of these characters in the story help the reader to under-
> stand the larger issue involved in these concluding events.
> For besides the Egyptian, the exhausted two hundred, and
> the elders of Judah, one other character does not participate
> in the battle yet shares in its spoil: if the battle is between the

Philistines and Saul's army, the one left behind by the Philistines is David himself. Far from exculpating David from any part in the death of Saul and the defeat of the Israelites, the stories in chapters 29-31 do not shrink from placing responsibility for the death of Saul and the defeat of Israel upon the shoulders of David himself: apparently willing to go down (29:4) or up (29:9) in battle against Saul and his own people, David is constrained to return to Ziklag, and he is left behind as the climax approaches. Nevertheless, the Deuteronomist uses David's own law and statute to put the story in perspective. Having been left behind by the lords of the Philistines, David more than anyone else shares in the spoils resulting from Saul's death. In fact, both benefit and blame are laid at David's feet by his own words: "For as his share is who goes down to battle, so shall his share be who stays by the baggage; they shall share alike" (30:24). Most immediately, David bears the responsibility for Saul's death as surely as Saul would have for David's, had David died at the hands of the Philistines in chapter 18. ... The king who hid himself among the baggage when called upon to rule (10:22) is replaced by one who stays by the baggage (30:24) as he waits for a chance to rule.

CHAPTER 31

THE END OF AN ERA

Meanwhile, the Philistines were fighting against Israel. But the men of Israel fled before the Philistines, and those slain fell on Mount Gilboa. The Philistines edged closer to Saul and his sons. The Philistines struck down Jonathan, Abinadab, and Malchishua, the sons of Saul.

The battle against Saul was heavy. The archers found him, and he was critically wounded by the archers. Saul said to his weapons-carrier, "Draw your sword and pierce me with it—lest this uncircumcised bunch come and pierce me and make a toy of me." But the weapons-carrier was unwilling, for he was terrified. Then Saul took the sword, and fell upon it. When the weapons-carrier saw that Saul was dead, he also fell upon his sword, and he died with him. So Saul, his three sons, his weapons-carrier, and all his men died together on that day. When the men of Israel—those on the other side of the valley and those beyond the Jordan—saw that the Israelites had fled and that Saul and his sons were dead, they abandoned the cities and fled themselves. The Philistines then came, and lived in them.

The next day the Philistines came to strip the dead bodies, and they found Saul and his three sons fallen on Mount Gilboa. They cut off his head and stripped off his weapons. Then they sent to report the news throughout the land of the Philistines all around, in the temple of their idols and among their people. They put his weapons in the temple of Ashtaroth, and impaled his corpse on the wall of Beth-Shan.

But then the inhabitants of Jabesh-Gilead heard about what the Philistines did to Saul. So all their valiant warriors arose and journeyed all night long, and they took the corpses of Saul and his sons from the wall of Beth-Shan. They brought them to Jabesh, and burned them there. Then they took their bones and buried them under the tamarisk tree in Jabesh, and fasted for seven days.

POINTS FOR REFLECTION:

1. As I have translated it, notice that this chapter begins with a temporal indicator "Meanwhile." To reiterate the point made above, Hamilton (2001: 286) remarks: "While David is in the deep south fighting the Amalekites successfully (ch. 30), Saul is in the north (Mount Gilboa) fighting the Philistines unsuccessfully (ch. 31)." Comment on the significance of this chronological parallel, and respond to Miscall's (1986: 181) questions:

> Chapters 30 and 31 gain in poignancy and power if we regard their events as simultaneous. In the far south, David is anxious about his own and about spoil, while in the far north Saul and the Israelite army perish. The contrast is increased by the length of the chapters—thirty-one verses in chapter 30 to thirteen verses in chapter 31. The defeat of Israel is so devastating that the Philistines are able to seize and inhabit Transjordanian cities. Did David foresee this and avoid being engulfed by it? If so, is this a cowardly or realistic act?

2. How should the reader understand Saul "falling on his own sword"? Is this nobly courageous? Or is *he himself* guilty of sending

his (own) hand "against the LORD's anointed? How would an early audience have read this passage? What about the fact that Saul's sons (including Jonathan) fall with him? Does this underscore the tragedy? Does this intersect with Samuel's prophetic word(s) about the "non-dynasty" of Saul? How should one interpret the weapons-carrier dying along with his master, Saul?

3. Evaluate Saul's last words, and compare it with some of his earlier utterances. Barbara Green (2003: 112-13) suggests that Saul seems more decisive here than at any more recent point. Is this the case? Green notes a final irony for King Saul: "It is his final asking, a last request that someone else resolve his life for him. But, so typically, his request is met with a refusal. The armor-bearer, as we have already heard stressed in chapters 24-26, likely knows better than—fears and refuses—to raise a hand against YHWH's anointed." Further, are there any similarities between the death of Saul and the death of Goliath in chapter 17? Note that each dies courtesy of his own sword, and each has his head removed by the enemy. Does this enhance the words of David's requiem in 2 Samuel 1, "How the mighty have fallen"?

4. As the reader finally evaluates the characterization of Israel's first king, consider this question: Is Saul a *tragic hero*? To paraphrase Aristotle's *Poetics*, a tragic character is essentially a good person, certainly not wholly evil. However, there is one "tragic flaw," a weakness, or a moment of misfortune (that may or may not be the hero's fault) that plunges the hero into ruin. This flaw may be a moment of self-doubt, or a character deficiency that functions as an "Achilles' heel." According to Aristotle, a tragedy involves "the situation of the man of much glory and good fortune who is not [too] superior in excellence and uprightness and yet does not come into his misfortune because of baseness and rascality but through

some inadequacy or positive fault" (Poetics, 2.13). There is, in other words, a combination of guilt *and* innocence if a character is truly "tragic." If the character is evil, then he/she cannot be a tragic figure according to this definition; there must be some measure of innocence and disastrous circumstance that is not wholly the character's fault. Keeping these criteria in mind, is Saul a tragic figure, or does he deserve everything he gets? Granted, the office of kingship perhaps never should have been created in the first place, and Saul certainly does not appear to have applied for the position. So, is there a combination of guilt *and* innocence in Saul's decline? Or do his character deficiencies immediately disqualify him from the job of king? Is it even possible to think of Saul in terms of *tragedy*, or is this an imposition of a different literary category onto this narrative? Does the portrait of Saul invite the reader to consider the theological doctrine of "non-election"? Evaluate this assessment of Saul's rise and fall by Gerhard von Rad (1962: 324-25):

> Thus, at an early time Saul was certainly on everyone's lips, and he also soon became a subject of poetry. But to faith his supreme interest was as the anointed who slipped from Jahweh's hand, the one quitting the stage, and yielding to him who was coming; that is, Saul as the God-forsaken, driven from one delusion to the other, desperate, and in the end swallowed up in miserable darkness. Right to the end the stories follow the unhappy king on his way with a deep human sympathy, and unfold a tragedy which in its final act rises to solemn grandeur. Actually, Israel never again gave birth to a poetic production which in certain of its features has such a close affinity with the spirit of Greek tragedy.

5. J. P. Fokkelman (1986: 628-29) notes a number of connections between chapter 11 (Saul's first episode as king, where he rescues

Jabesh-Gilead and is victorious over the Ammonites) and this final episode of Saul's career in chapter 31. First, Nahash threatens to mutilate the people of Jabesh-Gilead, just as Saul fears mutilation at the hands of the Philistines here in chapter 31. Second, Saul begins the rescue of the city of Jabesh-Gilead just as the "night watch" comes to an end, and likewise the warriors of Jabesh-Gilead journey "all night long" to rescue Saul from the Philistine temple. Third, Nahash had given Jabesh-Gilead seven days to find a "deliverer" in chapter 11, and likewise they fast for "seven days" in honor of their fallen deliverer in chapter 31. Fokkelman concludes:

> Thus there are all kinds of connecting lines between Saul's last war operation and his first. The Jabeshites have remained grateful to him and now carry out a dangerous lightning operation in enemy territory to save whatever can be saved. To that extent, (a part of) Saul's last wish is still fulfilled, his body is removed from the hands of the uncircumcised brutes and he is even given a burial, something of essential importance to the soul of the ancient Israelite and in contrast with the fate of being ignominiously hung on a wall. Thus respect and loyal treatment of Saul's body by friends contrasts with sacrilege and ill-treatment by the enemy.

6. Is it appropriate that one of the last words on King Saul goes to the inhabitants of Jabesh-Gilead? Does it appear that they never forget Saul's finest hour, his bravery and Spirit-empowered victory over Nahash "the snake" and his Ammonite eye-gougers in 1 Samuel 11? What is the literary impact of 1 Samuel ending on this note? It would seem that the people of Jabesh-Gilead first cleanse Saul's body through fire, and then give him a proper funeral. If Saul's career is a case study in failure, why does the narrator present this touching moment as the final action of the story? Miscall

(1986: 182) comments: "Saul's end is ignominious, yet the book of 1 Samuel closes by putting aside allusions to Saul's dark and clouded days. It closes with an act that is not a power play, a calculated show of restraint, a deception, or an attempt to buy someone's loyalty; it closes with pathos, with a memory of Saul's finest hour." Despite the courage of the Jabesh soldiers, they are obviously unable to recover the head of King Saul, and as Robert Polzin discusses at length, the term "head" is symbolic of kingship and leadership in Israel. Saul of course is "a head taller" than the rest of Israel; now that his head is removed, he is presumably the same size. Consider John Jarick's (2002: 84) comments:

> It is also worthy of note that the head of Saul had been taken away by and presumably remains with the Philistines; it is his body that the warriors of Jabesh are able to bury. The head of Israel's quasi-king is not mentioned again. David will later achieve success over the Philistines, but he does not bring back Saul's head. The house of Saul will never again rule Israel; that "head" is now out of the way, and the scene is set for David to be elevated to the throne.

7. The book of 1 Samuel is part of a larger work. How does this ending relate to both what comes before (e.g. the book of Judges) and what is to come (e.g. the book of 2 Samuel)? Evaluate the following comment of McCarter (1980: 443-44): "The report of Saul's death is remarkable for its lack of finality. To be sure, Saul is gone now—and also Jonathan, his heir—and the Gibeah episode in the history of the Israelite monarchy is over forever. But the new king is not yet on the throne, and an atmosphere of incompleteness surrounds the account of the battle of Mount Gilboa and its aftermath. The larger narrative to which this passage belongs has, as we have seen, two major themes, viz. the demise of Saul and the rise of David. Only the former is completed now." Furthermore, if

1 Samuel is part of a continuous narrative from Joshua to 2 Kings, what difference does this make for one's reading? Paul House (1998: 236) notes, "This initial instance of kingship foreshadows God's assessment of every future king in the book of Kings." What kind of foreshadowing does the reader sense for the monarchy in Israel? Finally, comment on what Rolf Knierim (1978: 20-51) refers to as "The Messianic Concept of the First Book of Samuel." Do you sense any messianic undercurrents in 1 Samuel? (See further Satterthwaite [1995: 41-65] and Polak [1994: 119-47]). If so, how would you articulate such a messianic dimension, and how does this integrate with a larger biblical theology?

BIBLIOGRAPHY

James S. Ackerman, "Who Can Stand before YHWH, This Holy God? A Reading of 1 Samuel 1-15." *Prooftexts* 11 (1991) 1-24.

Peter R. Ackroyd, *The First Book of Samuel: Commentary*. New York: Cambridge University Press, 1971.

Robert Alter, *The Art of Biblical Narrative*. New York: Basic Books, 1981.

Robert Alter, *The World of Biblical Literature*. London: SPCK, 1992.

Robert Alter, *The David Story: A Translation with Commentary of 1 & 2 Samuel*. New York: Norton, 1999.

Yairah Amit, *Reading Biblical Narratives: Literary Criticism and the Hebrew Bible*. Translated by Yael Lotan. Minneapolis: Fortress, 2001.

Joyce G. Baldwin, *I and II Samuel: An Introduction and Commentary*. Downers Grove, Ill.: InterVarsity Press, 1988.

Robert D. Bergen, *1, 2 Samuel*. Nashville: Broadman & Holman, 1996.

Walter Brueggemann, *First and Second Samuel*. Louisville, Ky.: John Knox Press, 1990.

David J. A. Clines and Tamara C. Eskenazi, eds. *Telling Queen Michal's Story: An Experiment in Comparative Interpretation*. Sheffield: Sheffield Academic Press, 1992.

Kenneth M. Craig Jr., "Rhetorical Aspects of Questions Answered with Silence in 1 Samuel 14:37 and 28:6." *Catholic Biblical Quarterly*

56 (1994) 221-239.

Lyle M. Eslinger, Kingship of God in Crisis: *A Close Reading of 1 Samuel 1-12*. Sheffield: Almond Press, 1985.

Craig A. Evans, "David in the Dead Sea Scrolls." Pp. 183-197 in *The Scrolls and the Scriptures: Qumran Fifty Years After,* ed. S. Porter and others; Sheffield, England: Sheffield Academic Press, 1997.

Jan P. Fokkelman, *Narrative Art and Poetry in the Books of Samuel. Vol. 2, The Crossing Fates* (1 Sam. 13-31 and 2 Sam. 1). Assen: Van Gorcum, 1986.

Jan P. Fokkelman, *Narrative Art and Poetry in the Books of Samuel. Vol. 4, Vow and Desire* (1 Sam. 1-12). Assen: Van Gorcum, 1993.

Everett Fox, *Give Us A King!* New York: Schocken, 1999.

Terence E. Fretheim, "Divine Foreknowledge, Divine Constancy, and the Rejection of Saul's Kingship." *CBQ* 47 (1985) 595-602.

Moshe Garsiel, *The First Book of Samuel: A Literary Study of Comparative Structures, Analogies, Parallels.* Ramat Gan, Israel: Revivim, 1985.

Robert P. Gordon, *1 & 2 Samuel.* Exeter: Paternoster, 1986.

Barbara Green, *Mikhail Bakhtin and Biblical Scholarship: An Introduction.* Atlanta: Society of Biblical Literature, 2000.

Barbara Green, *King Saul's Asking.* Collegeville: Liturgical Press, 2003

David M. Gunn, *The Story of King David.* Sheffield: JSOT Press, 1978.

Scott J. Hafemann, ed., *Biblical Theology: Retrospect and Prospect.* Downers Grove, Ill.: InterVarsity Press, 2002.

Baruch Halpern, *David's Secret Demons: Messiah, Murderer, Traitor, King.* Grand Rapids: Eerdmans, 2001.

Victor P. Hamilton, *Handbook on the Historical Books.* Grand Rapids: Baker, 2001.

Paul R. House, *Old Testament Theology.* Downers Grove, Ill.: InterVarsity Press, 1998.

David M. Howard, Jr., "The Transfer of Power from Saul to David in 1 Sam 16:13-14." *Journal of the Evangelical Theological Society* 32 (1989) 473-483.

W. Lee Humphreys, "From Tragic Hero to Villain: A Study of the Figure of Saul and the Development of 1 Samuel." *Journal for the Study of the Old Testament* 22 (1982) 95-117.

John Jarick, *1 Chronicles.* London: Sheffield Academic Press, 2002. .

David Jobling, *1 Samuel.* Collegeville: Liturgical Press, 1998.

John Kessler, "Sexuality and Politics: The Motif of the Displaced Husband in the books of Samuel." *Catholic Biblical Quarterly* 62 (2000) 409-23.

Ralph W. Klein, *1 Samuel.* Waco, Texas: Word, 1983.

Rolf Knierim, "The Messianic Concept of the First Book of Samuel." Pp. 20-51 in *Jesus and the Historian,* ed. F. T. Trotter. Philadelphia: Westminster, 1978.

Peter J. Leithart, "Nabal and his Wine." *Journal of Biblical Literature* 120 (2001) 525-27.

V. Philips Long, *The Reign and Rejection of King Saul: A Case for Literary and Theological Coherence.* Atlanta: Scholars Press, 1989.

Peter Kyle McCarter, *I Samuel: A New Translation with Introduction, Notes and Commentary.* Garden City, N.Y.: Doubleday, 1980.

Peter D. Miscall, *1 Samuel: A Literary Reading.* Bloomington: Indiana University Press, 1986.

Eugene H. Peterson, *First and Second Samuel.* Louisville, KY: Westminster John Knox Press, 1999.

Frank Polak, "David's Kingship—A Precarious Equilibrium." Pp. 119-47 in *Politics and Theopolitics in the Bible and Postbiblical Literature,* eds. Henning Graf Reventlow Yair Hoffman, and Benjamin Uffenheimer. Sheffield: Sheffield Academic Press, 1994.

Robert Polzin, *Samuel and the Deuteronomist.* Bloomington: Indiana University Press, 1993.

211

O. H. Prouser, "Suited to the Throne: The Symbolic Use of Clothing in the David and Saul Narratives." *Journal for the Study of the Old Testament* 71 (1996) 27-37.

Gerhard von Rad, *Old Testament Theology I: The Theology of Israel's Historical Traditions.* Translated by D. N. G. Stalker. New York: Harper & Row, 1962.

Gary A. Rendsburg, "Confused Language as a Deliberate Literary Device in Biblical Hebrew Narrative." *Journal of Hebrew Scriptures,* volume 2 (1999), www.purl.org/jhs.

Pamela Tamarkin Reis, "Collusion at Nob: A New Reading of 1 Samuel 21-22." *Journal for the Study of the Old Testament* 61 (1994) 59-73.

Joel Rosenberg, "1 and 2 Samuel." Pp. 122-45 in *The Literary Guide to the Bible.* Robert Alter and Frank Kermode, eds. Cambridge: Harvard University Press, 1987.

Joel Rosenberg, King and Kin: *Political Allegory in the Hebrew Bible.* Bloomington: Indiana University Press, 1986.

Philip E. Satterthwaite, "David in the Books of Samuel: A Messianic Expectation?" Pp. 41-65 in *The Lord's Anointed: Interpretation of Old Testament Messianic Texts.* Philip E. Satterthwaite, Richard S. Hess, and Gordon J. Wenham, eds. Grand Rapids: Baker, 1995.

Frank Spina, "A Prophet's 'Pregnant Pause': Samuel's Silence in the Ark Narrative (1 Samuel 4:1-7:12)." *Horizons in Biblical Theology* 13 (1991) 59-73.

Frank Spina, "Eli's Seat: The Transition from Priest to Prophet in 1 Samuel 1-4." *Journal for the Study of the Old Testament* 62 (1994) 67-75.

Meir Sternberg, *The Poetics of Biblical Narrative: Ideological Literature and the Drama of Reading.* Bloomington: Indiana University Press, 1985.

Eugene C. Ulrich, *The Qumran Text of Samuel and Josephus.* Missoula, MT: Scholars Press, 1978.

Printed in the United States
18351LVS00004B/28-30